THE BIBLE

THE EPIC BATTLE

*God and Lucifer's battle for the position of
"Most High God" possessor of heaven and earth*

Greg Todd

A fascinating look at God's two-fold strategy to
reconcile all things, both in heaven and earth,
to the headship of the Lord Jesus Christ

ISBN 978-1-63630-687-2 (Paperback)
ISBN 978-1-63630-688-9 (Digital)

A special thanks to John and Sherry
Verstagen, for their contributions.

Covenant Books, Inc.
11661 Hwy 707
Murrells Inlet, SC 29576
www.covenantbooks.com

A fascinating overview of God's plans and purpose to reconcile all things, both in heaven and earth, to the headship of the Lord Jesus Christ, "the blessed and only Potentate, the King of kings and Lord of lords"

—1 Timothy 6:15

CONTENTS

PREFACE

Most of us don't think about God, religion or the Bible as this EPIC battle going on in the unseen world between this ugly beast of an image representing evil and this blue-eyed, fair skin, long-haired Jewish prophet at best, imposter at worst. Truth is, they really have been engaged in this battle since the beginning of time as we know it. The battle is for total rulership over heaven and earth otherwise known as the "Most High God". The Epic Battle allows you to see God's amazing strategy that will lead Him to victory over both dominions.

Let's set the stage for this epic battle between good and evil that being God and Lucifer. In the beginning God created the heaven and the earth. God also created angelic beings in heavenly places that would serve and worship him. One such angel was Lucifer. Lucifer is said to be the most beautiful, most gifted, and most powerful of all God's angelic creation. As a matter of fact God appointed Lucifer as the "anointed cherub" keeper of the throne room of God. Unfortunately this exalted position was not good enough for Lucifer, rather he wanted to be "like" the Most High God ruler of heaven and earth and the only god worthy to be worshipped. How exactly did Satan lay claim to his attempted takeover of God. First Satan "trafficked" a lie to the other angels that he was wiser than God and that no secret could be kept from him. God, in his infinite wisdom told Satan that he would take him in his own "craftiness" by keeping a secret from Him (the Mystery}. The Epic Battle lays out the details of God's strategy and Satan's counter strategy throughout the ages that will end in God's victory.

For most Christians, the Bible seems to be a little confusing and quite daunting to understand. So often for the small percentage of Christians that actually want to understand the Bible, they really just don't understand how God designed it and how the books are laid out according to God's actual design. Unfortunately, today most Christians read more books about the Bible than they do the Bible itself, never gaining a full appreciation for this supernaturally inspired and preserved Word of God. The Bible contains sixty-six books that were not assembled in the chronological order in which they were breathed by God and penned by man. It contains thirty-nine Old Testament books and twenty-seven New Testament books. Man decided what books he would call the New Testament. The Bible actually says that a Testament could not be written while the Testator was alive (Heb. 9:16–17). So according to God, most of the Gospels—Matthew, Mark, Luke, and John—were written while Christ was alive.

Hmmm, why is that? The Bible is a big book; it is all for us, but it is not all about or to us today. We need to understand how we fit in to the amazing plans God has laid out in His written word of God. There is only one verse in the Bible that clearly instructs us on "how" we are to study the Bible. In 2 Timothy 2:15, the apostle Paul tells us to "rightly divide the word of truth." It is clear by this statement from God that we can make "wrong" divisions and therefore misapply scripture that is not intended for us today as doctrine or direct instruction for the believer today. This study will help you understand "why" God laid out the book in the way He did. It will finally address seeming contradictions that many Christians come across and then end up confused as to what is actually correct. A very important one is the distinction between Romans 4:5 vs. James 2:24, where one says you are saved by faith alone and the other says that without additional works your faith alone is not counted for righteousness. Which is it? Where most folks get confused is when reading and trying to apply the truths in the Gospels: Mathew, Mark, Luke, and John. Modern scholars have coined this the "New Testament," yet as you will see in this book, scripture reveals that the Gospels are not "to" or directly about the body of Christ.

The Bible: The Epic Battle was written to help provide a broad overview of what the Bible is all about and, therefore, how the "pieces" fit together perfectly and amazingly to unfold God's eternal plans and purpose.

Understanding the epic battle will provide answers to several questions that have puzzled many Christians. Here are a few examples:

- "Ask, and it will be given to you; seek, and you will find; knock, and it will be opened to you" (Matt. 7:7). Why does this not work for us today?
- "And these signs will follow those who believe…casting out devils, speaking in new tongues, take up serpents, drink anything deadly…" (Mark 16:17). Really?
- Why did Jesus Christ say, "I am not sent but unto the lost sheep of the house of Israel" (Matt. 15:24)?
- What is "the preaching of Jesus Christ, **according to the revelation of the mystery**" (Rom. 16:25)?
- What are the two distinct messages that are referenced in Acts 3:21 vs. Romans 16:25?
- Why does Romans 4:5 say, "To him that **worketh not**, but believeth on him that justifieth the ungodly, his faith is counted for righteousness" while James 2:24 says, "**By works** a man is justified and not by faith only"?
- Why Paul? While on earth, Jesus Christ chose twelve apostles because there are twelve tribes of Israel (Matt. 19:28). When Judas fell, Matthias was chosen to take his place. Why, then, did the risen, ascended Lord Jesus Christ reach down to save and call Paul to be an apostle?

Scripture Verses

Matthew 7:7

Ask, and it shall be given you; seek, and ye shall find; knock, and it shall be opened unto you.

Mark 16:17–18

And these signs shall follow them that believe; In my name shall they cast out devils; they shall speak with new tongues;

They shall take up serpents; and if they drink any deadly thing, it shall not hurt them; they shall lay hands on the sick, and they shall recover.

Matthew 15:34

But he answered and said, I am not sent but unto the lost sheep of the house of Israel.

Romans 16:25

Now to him that is of power to stablish you according to my gospel, and the preaching of Jesus Christ, according to the revelation of the mystery, which was kept secret since the world began.

Acts 3:21

Whom the heaven must receive until the times of restitution of all things, which God hath spoken by the mouth of all his holy prophets since the world began.

Romans 4:5

But to him that worketh not, but believeth on him that justifieth the ungodly, his faith is counted for righteousness.

James 2:24

Ye see then how that by works a man is justified, and not by faith only.

Matthew 19:28

And Jesus said unto them, Verily I say unto you, That ye which have followed me, in the regeneration when the Son of man shall sit in the throne of his glory, ye also shall sit upon twelve thrones, judging the twelve tribes of Israel.

OUR PRAYER

A s you read, we pray that you will be like the noble Bereans who "received the word with all readiness of mind, and searched the scriptures daily, whether those things were so" (Acts 17:11). That your faith would be strengthened and your understanding of how we fit into God's eternal plans would be clear.

All verses used are from the King James Version of the Bible. Their references appear at the bottom of each page. We have incorporated all footnoted scriptures along with note pages for every section. If time permits, feel free to compare any/all scriptures from KJV to any other version you may be familiar with.

Note: In some of the verses quoted, the author has placed words in bold letters for emphasis. The bolding is the author's. It is not in the KJV. However, words that appear in italics are words that are italicized in the KJV.

INTRODUCTION

The Bible (Scripture) is God's eternal, inspired word. Psalm 119:89 and Daniel 10:21[1] teach that it was settled in heaven before it was ever written on earth. God's Word guides all that God does. By it "the worlds were framed" (Heb. 11:3), and in it is God's offer of eternal life to those who will believe it.

God's Word is His revelation to us of Himself. We know God through His word. The central person of the Bible is the Lord Jesus Christ, the living Word of God (John 1:1). He is pictured in some way in every one of its books. Hebrews 10:7 says, "In the volume of the book it is written of me." He is the seed of the woman, the great high priest, the "Most High God" in ages to come, the Passover lamb, the kinsman redeemer, the rock of salvation, the chief cornerstone, the seed of David, the great "I am," the Son of God, the head of the church, and so much more. Jesus Christ is also rightfully "the blessed and only Potentate, the King of kings, and Lord of lords" of all things—both in heaven and on earth (1 Tim. 6:15; Col. 1:16).

However, since Lucifer's fall, there has been rebellion in *both* realms of God's kingdom. The Bible reveals God's twofold plan to end the rebellion, "that at the name of Jesus every knee should bow, of *things* in heaven and *things* in earth, and *things* under the earth" (Phil. 2:10). Through Israel—the nation God created and will one day redeem—He will reclaim the earth. Through the body He is cur-

---

[1] An angel told Daniel that he would show him "that which is noted in the scripture of truth." Daniel recorded what the angel told him, and those words become part of the Bible. Daniel 11 was already written in heaven before Daniel wrote it down on earth!

rently creating—"the body of Christ"[2]—He will reclaim the heavenly places.

Thus, "in the dispensation of the fullness of times," He will "gather together in one **all things in Christ, both which are in heaven, and which are on earth**."[3] This is the eternal purpose and twofold plan of God revealed in the Bible. *The "Epic Battle" is a big picture view of God's plan for the ages* written to help you see how and where *you* fit into the outworking of His plan.

---

[2]   Daniel 10:21.
[3]   Ephesians 1:10.

Scripture Verses

Psalm 119:89

Forever, O Lord,

Your word is settled in heaven.

Daniel 10:21

But I will shew thee that which is noted in the scripture of truth: and there is none that holdeth with me in these things, but Michael your prince.

John 1:1

In the beginning was the Word, and the Word was with God, and the Word was God.

1 Timothy 6:15

Which in his times he shall shew, who is the blessed and only Potentate, the King of kings, and Lord of lords.

Colossians 1:16

For by him were all things created, that are in heaven, and that are in earth, visible and invisible, whether they be thrones, or dominions, or principalities, or powers: all things were created by him, and for him.

Philippians 2:10

That at the name of Jesus every knee should bow, of things in heaven, and things in earth, and things under the earth.

1 Corinthians 12:27

Now ye are the body of Christ, and members in particular.

Ephesians 1:10

That in the dispensation of the fulness of times he might gather together in one all things in Christ, both which are in heaven, and which are on earth; even in him.

Salvation

"Rightly Dividing the Word of Truth"

Seeing how and where *you* fit into the outworking of God's plan is vital because, while all the Bible is *for us*, it is not all *to* us or *about* us. We cannot open the Bible and apply any and all verses to ourselves. For example, many passages command animal sacrifices. Obviously, no true Christian would teach that we should offer animal sacrifices today. Exodus 31:15 says whosoever does any work on the Sabbath day he shall surely be put to death. We know that this does not apply to us *today*, but exactly why? Mathew 24:19 says "And woe unto them that are with child, and to them that suck in those days!" Now, let's compare this with 1 Timothy 5:15, "I will therefore that younger women marry, bear children, guide the house, give none occasion to the adversary to speak reproachfully." Ok, which is it? Is is good to have kids or not? We must distinguish between verses that apply today and verses that do not. We must "rightly divide the word of truth" (2 Tim. 2:15).

Understanding "the epic battle" and God's twofold plan will help us do this.

In no other area is "rightly dividing" more important than it is in understanding how to be saved from hell and stand completely forgiven and justified before a holy God. From cover to cover, the Bible teaches that salvation is by faith in God's Word, for "without faith it is impossible to please Him" (Heb. 11:6), and "faith cometh by hearing and hearing by the word of God" (Rom. 10:17). Saving faith is always a positive response to God's *revealed* word. However, God's revealed word has not always been the same in every age. So it is imperative that you know what His word is *to you*!

18

Time Past

The shed blood of Christ is the payment for the sins of all men of all ages. No one, in any age, could ever be saved except by the shed blood of Christ. However, in time past, prior to the cross, people did not know this. God had not revealed it yet, so their faith had to be placed in God's revealed word to them *at that time.* When it was, God looked ahead to the cross in order to forgive their sins (Rom. 3:25).

According to Hebrews 11, by faith Abel offered a sacrifice, Noah prepared an ark, Abraham left his land and offered up Isaac, and Moses forsook Egypt. Clearly, Israelites living under the law could not have had true faith in God and at the same time refuse to offer the sacrifices commanded in the law. The sacrifices did not save them, but they were the evidence of their faith in God's revealed word to them. In time past, then, faith was manifest by works.

"But Now" (Romans 3:21)

Today, though, God's WORD tells us that we are not under the law, but under grace (Rom. 6:14). God has revealed to us who live after the cross that Christ has done all the work necessary to save us—He shed His blood as the full payment for all of our sins, died, and rose again as proof that God has accepted the payment (Rom. 3:21–28 and 4:25). Today God tells us to *stop working* for salvation and trust in the work of His son for our justification:

> But to him that **worketh not**, but **believeth**
> **on him** that justifieth the ungodly, his faith is
> counted for righteousness. (Rom. 4:5)

True faith today, then, will be manifest by resting in the shed blood of Christ, and that *alone*, for justification. Adding works of any kind (water baptism, committing your life to Christ, walking an aisle, keeping the law, repeated confession of sins...) to the work of Christ *in order to obtain forgiveness or salvation* is a denial that *His* work is enough. It is simply faith in God's good news in this age of grace.

Ages to Come

What about in the future? This age of grace will not last forever. One day the church, the body of Christ, will be taken home to heaven, and God will have another message for the world—one that will again require works, such as not taking the mark of the beast (Rev. 14:12). But this will be much clearer after reading *The Bible— The Epic Battle.*

Scripture Verses

1 Timothy 2:15

Study to shew thyself approved unto God, a workman that needeth not to be ashamed, rightly dividing the word of truth. (KJV)

Hebrews 11:6

But without faith it is impossible to please him: for he that cometh to God must believe that he is, and that he is a rewarder of them that diligently seek him.

Romans 10:17

So then faith cometh by hearing, and hearing by the word of God.

Romans 3:21-27

But now the righteousness of God apart from the law is revealed, being witnessed by the Law and the Prophets, even the righteousness of God, through faith in Jesus Christ, to all and on all who believe. For there is no difference; for all have sinned and fall short of the glory of God, being justified freely by His grace through the redemption that is in Christ Jesus, whom God set forth as a propitiation by His blood, through faith, to demonstrate His righteousness, because in His forbearance God had passed over the sins that were previously committed, to demonstrate at the present time His righteousness, that He might be just and the justifier of the one who has faith in Jesus. Where is boasting then? It is excluded. By what law? Of works? No, but by the law of faith. Therefore we conclude that a man is justified by faith apart from the deeds of the law.

Romans 4:25

Who was delivered for our offences, and was raised again for our justification.

Romans 6:14

For sin shall not have dominion over you: for ye are not under the law, but under grace.

CREATION: BY AND FOR CHRIST

T he Bible begins by telling us that God created the heaven and the earth. Note that throughout the Bible, these two realms are distinct. When speaking of creation, God does not use the word *universe* but, instead, specifies "the heaven and the earth."[4]

We learn that God created all things in heaven and on earth by and for His son, the Lord Jesus Christ. The "all things" include "thrones, dominions, principalities, and powers."[5] Jesus Christ was, and is, to be "the blessed and only Potentate, the King of kings, and Lord of lords" over all of creation, both in heaven and earth.[6] (Even in the eternal state, the distinction between heaven and earth will remain in "a new heaven and a new earth."[7])

In the beginning, God created the heavens and the earth

---

4 Genesis 1:1; Ephesians 3:15.
5 Colossians 1:16.
6 1 Timothy 6:15; Philippians 2:10; Ephesians 1:10; Colossians 1:16–20.
7 Revelation 21:1; Isaiah 65:17; 2 Peter 3:13.

Scripture Verses

Genesis 1:1

In the beginning God created the heaven and the earth.

Ephesians 3:15

Of whom the whole family in heaven and earth is named.

Colossians 1:16

For by him were all things created, that are in heaven, and that are in earth, visible and invisible, whether they be thrones, or dominions, or principalities, or powers: all things were created by him, and for him.

1 Timothy 6:15

Which in his times he shall shew, who is the blessed and only Potentate, the King of kings, and Lord of lords.

Philippians 2:10

That at the name of Jesus every knee should bow, of things in heaven, and things in earth, and things under the earth.

Ephesians 1:10

That in the dispensation of the fulness of times he might gather together in one all things in Christ, both which are in heaven, and which are on earth; even in him.

Colossians 1:16–20

For by him were all things created, that are in heaven, and that are in earth, visible and invisible, whether they be thrones, or dominions, or principalities, or powers: all things were created by him, and for him: And he is before all things, and by him all things consist. And he is the head of the body, the church: who is the beginning, the firstborn from the dead; that in all things he might have the preeminence. For it pleased the Father that in him should all fulness dwell; And, having made peace through the blood of his cross, by him to reconcile all things unto himself; by him, I say, whether they be things in earth, or things in heaven.

Revelation 21:1

And I saw a new heaven and a new earth: for the first heaven and the first earth were passed away; and there was no more sea.

Isaiah 65:17

"For, behold, I create new heavens and a new earth: and the former shall not be remembered, nor come into mind."

2 Peter 3:13

Nevertheless we, according to his promise, look for new heavens and a new earth, wherein dwelleth righteousness.

LUCIFER—"I WILL"

However, one of God's creatures did not like God's plan. His name was Lucifer. Lucifer was "the anointed cherub that covereth."[8] He was created to lead the angelic host in song and praise to God. He was covered with beautiful stones that reflected the glory of God throughout the heavens.[9] His position was higher than any other created being, but Lucifer was not satisfied. He wanted to be "like the most High."[10]

Genesis 14:19 and 22 define the title, "the most high God," as the title that speaks of God being "the possessor of heaven and earth." Satan wanted to possess heaven and earth. His pride caused his fall, and he became Satan, the devil.

---

[8]   Ezekiel 28:13.
[9]   Ezekiel 28:14.
[10]   Isaiah 14:12–15.

Ezekiel 28:13

Thou hast been in Eden the garden of God; every precious stone was thy covering, the sardius, topaz, and the diamond, the beryl, the onyx, and the jasper, the sapphire, the emerald, and the carbuncle, and gold: the workmanship of thy tabrets and of thy pipes was prepared in thee in the day that thou wast created.

Ezekiel 28:14

Thou art the anointed cherub that covereth; and I have set thee so: thou wast upon the holy mountain of God; thou hast walked up and down in the midst of the stones of fire.

Isaiah 14:12–15

How you are fallen from heaven, O Lucifer, son of the morning! How you are cut down to the ground, You who weakened the nations! For you have said in your heart: "I will ascend into heaven, I will exalt my throne above the stars of God; I will also sit on the mount of the congregation On the farthest sides of the north; I will ascend above the heights of the clouds, I will be like the Most High." Yet you shall be brought down to Sheol, To the lowest depths of the Pit.

Genesis 14:19, 22

And he blessed him, and said, Blessed be Abram of the most high God, possessor of heaven and earth: And Abram said to the king of Sodom, I have lift up mine hand unto the LORD, the most high God, the possessor of heaven and earth.

NOTES

REBELLION IN HEAVEN

Since his fall, Satan's plan has been to take control of all creation. He led a rebellion in heaven, and many angels followed him.[11] God says the heavens are unclean in His sight.[12] (God prepared hell for these fallen angels.[13])

Since God knew beforehand that Lucifer would rebel, He had a plan to one day cleanse the heavens and restore them to the headship of the Lord Jesus Christ.

However, he kept His plan to do so secret so that Satan and his princes would not know it.[14] God did not reveal His plan to restore the *heavenly places* anywhere in the Old Testament, so we will not discover it until much later in the Bible. For now, just remember that God did have a secret plan to regain complete control of the heavenly places, but He would only make it known in due time.

---

11   Revelation 12:9; Ephesians 6:12.
12   Matthew 25:41–43.
13   2 Peter 2:4.
14   1 Corinthians 2:6–8; Ephesians 3:8–10.

Scripture Verses

Revelation 12:9

And the great dragon was cast out, that old serpent, called the Devil, and Satan, which deceiveth the whole world: he was cast out into the earth, and his angels were cast out with him.

Ephesians 6:12

For we do not wrestle against flesh and blood, but against principalities, against powers, against the rulers of the darkness of this age, against spiritual hosts of wickedness in the heavenly places.

Matthew 25:41–43

Then He will also say to those on the left hand, "Depart from Me, you cursed, into the everlasting fire prepared for the devil and his angels: for I was hungry and you gave Me no food; I was thirsty and you gave Me no drink; I was a stranger and you did not take Me in, naked and you did not clothe Me, sick and in prison and you did not visit Me."

2 Peter 2:4

For if God spared not the angels that sinned, but cast them down to hell, and delivered them into chains of darkness, to be reserved unto judgment.

1 Corinthians 2:6–8

However, we speak wisdom among those who are mature, yet not the wisdom of this age, nor of the rulers of this age, who are coming to nothing. But we speak the wisdom of God in a mystery, the hidden wisdom which God ordained before the ages for our glory, which none of the rulers of this age knew; for had they known, they would not have crucified the Lord of glory.

Ephesians 3:8–10

To me, who am less than the least of all the saints, this grace was given, that I should preach among the Gentiles the unsearchable riches of Christ, and to make all see what is the fellowship of the mystery, which from the beginning of the ages has been hidden in God who created all things through Jesus Christ; to the intent that now the manifold wisdom of God might be made known by the church to the principalities and powers in the heavenly places.

NOTES

REBELLION ON EARTH

When God created Adam and Eve, he instructed them to have dominion over the earth. Satan sought to continue his rebellion there. God had given Adam one simple command, "Of the tree of the knowledge of good and evil, thou shalt not eat of it: for in the day that thou eatest thereof thou shalt surely die."[15]

Satan, the serpent, questioned God's word by asking, "Yea, hath God said…?"[16] Then he challenged God's word by lying, "Ye shall not surely die."[17]

Instead of trusting God's word, Adam and Eve ate of the fruit. Thus, they brought sin and death into the world, and the earth was placed under a curse.[18] Because of this, Satan was able to take dominion of the earth from Adam.[19]

But this did not take God by surprise either. Just as God had a plan to take back the heavens, he had a plan to take back the earth. However, he *did* begin to reveal His plan for *the earth*, little by little, right from the beginning of the world.[20] This is what we read about in the Old Testament. The Old Testament covenants and prophecies reveal God's eternal plans *for the earth*.

---

[15] Genesis 2:17.

[16] Genesis 3:1.

[17] Genesis 3:4.

[18] Genesis 3:16–19; Romans 5:12.

[19] Luke 4:5–6; John 14:30;
2 Corinthians 4:4.

[20] Luke 1:70; Acts 3:21.

Genesis 2:17

But of the tree of the knowledge of good and evil, thou shalt not eat of it: for in the day that thou eatest thereof thou shalt surely die.

Genesis 3:1

Now the serpent was more subtil than any beast of the field which the LORD God had made. And he said unto the woman, Yea, hath God said, Ye shall not eat of every tree of the garden?

Genesis 3:4

And the serpent said unto the woman, Ye shall not surely die.

Genesis 3:16

Unto the woman he said, I will greatly multiply thy sorrow and thy conception; in sorrow thou shalt bring forth children; and thy desire shall be to thy husband, and he shall rule over thee.

Romans 5:12

Wherefore, as by one man sin entered into the world, and death by sin; and so death passed upon all men, for that all have sinned.

Luke 4:5–6

Then the devil, taking Him up on a high mountain, showed Him all the kingdoms of the world in a moment of time. And the devil said to Him, "All this authority I will give You, and their glory; for this has been delivered to me, and I give it to whomever I wish."

John 14:30

Hereafter I will not talk much with you: for the prince of this world cometh, and hath nothing in me.

1 Corinthians 4:4

Whose minds the god of this age has blinded, who do not believe, lest the light of the gospel of the glory of Christ, who is the image of God, should shine on them.

Luke 1:70

As he spake by the mouth of his holy prophets, which have been since the world began.

Acts 3:21

Whom the heaven must receive until the times of restitution of all things, which God hath spoken by the mouth of all his holy prophets since the world began.

NOTES

_____
_____
_____
_____
_____
_____
_____
_____
_____
_____
_____
_____
_____
_____
_____
_____
_____
_____
_____
_____
_____
_____
_____
_____
_____
_____
_____
_____

THE OLD TESTAMENT
God's Plans to Redeem the Earth

THE SEED OF THE WOMAN

At the fall of man, God told the serpent (Satan) that his seed would bruise the heel of the seed of the woman, but her seed (meaning a man, not an angel) would eventually bruise his head.[21] We now know, from further revelation in God's Word, that the seed of the woman is Jesus Christ, who will one day destroy Satan.

But Jesus Christ did not come right away. God let men multiply on the earth.

As they did, Satan and his angels attempted to contaminate the human race in order to prevent the pure seed of the woman from coming.[22]

By Genesis 6, Satan had infected the human race so badly that only one man was "perfect in his generations."[23] So God sent a flood to destroy all of mankind except for Noah and his family. From Noah's family, the earth was repopulated,[24] and the promised seed of the woman would eventually be born.

---

[21] Genesis 3:15.
[22] Genesis 6:1–4.
[23] Genesis 6:9.
[24] Genesis 9:19.

Scripture Verses

Genesis 3:15

And I will put enmity between you and the woman, and between your seed and her Seed; He shall bruise your head, And you shall bruise His heel.

Genesis 6:1–4

And it came to pass, when men began to multiply on the face of the earth, and daughters were born unto them,

That the sons of God saw the daughters of men that they were fair; and they took them wives of all which they chose.

And the LORD said, My spirit shall not always strive with man, for that he also is flesh: yet his days shall be an hundred and twenty years.

There were giants in the earth in those days; and also after that, when the sons of God came in unto the daughters of men, and they bare children to them, the same became mighty men which were of old, men of renown.

Genesis 6:9

These are the generations of Noah: Noah was a just man and perfect in his generations, and Noah walked with God.

Genesis 9:19

These three were the sons of Noah, and from these the whole earth was populated.

NOTES

THE ABRAHAMIC COVENANT

DISTRIBUTION of the sons of CANAAN and their Descendants

Enlarged Scale

As men multiplied on the earth again, they soon became infected with Satan's idolatry and rebellion. God had told them to spread over all the earth; instead, "they said, Go to, let us build us a city and a tower, whose top *may reach* unto heaven; and let us make us a name lest we be scattered abroad upon the face of the whole earth" (Gen. 11:4).

So God confused their languages, and the earth became divided into nations. This is when God "gave them up" and "gave them over to a reprobate mind."[25]

At this point, God revealed a little more about His plan to regain the earth: He would make His *own special* nation from a man named Abram (Abraham). He would use this nation to bless all the other nations.[26] His nation would dwell in a special land, Canaan. He told Abraham the borders of the great kingdom his seed would one day have on this earth.[27]

---

[25]   Genesis 11:1–9 with Romans 1:24, 26, 28.
[26]   Genesis 12:1–3, 18:18.
[27]   Genesis 15:18–21, 17:8.

Remember this part of the covenant especially:

———— • ————

I will make of thee a great nation, and I will bless thee,
and make thy name great;
and thou shalt be a blessing: And I will bless them that bless thee,
and curse him that curseth thee:
and in thee shall all families of the earth be blessed.
(Gen. 12:1–3)

———— • ————

Scripture Verses

Genesis 11:1–9

And the whole earth was of one language, and of one speech.

And it came to pass, as they journeyed from the east, that they found a plain in the land of Shinar; and they dwelt there.

And they said one to another, Go to, let us make brick, and burn them thoroughly. And they had brick for stone, and slime had they for morter.

And they said, Go to, let us build us a city and a tower, whose top may reach unto heaven; and let us make us a name, lest we be scattered abroad upon the face of the whole earth.

And the LORD came down to see the city and the tower, which the children of men builded.

And the LORD said, Behold, the people is one, and they have all one language; and this they begin to do: and now nothing will be restrained from them, which they have imagined to do.

Go to, let us go down, and there confound their language, that they may not understand one another's speech.

So the LORD scattered them abroad from thence upon the face of all the earth: and they left off to build the city.

Therefore is the name of it called Babel; because the LORD did there confound the language of all the earth: and from thence did the LORD scatter them abroad upon the face of all the earth.

Romans 1:24, 26, 28

Wherefore God also gave them up to uncleanness through the lusts of their own hearts, to dishonour their own bodies between themselves:

For this cause God gave them up unto vile affections: for even their women did change the natural use into that which is against nature:

And even as they did not like to retain God in their knowledge, God gave them over to a reprobate mind, to do those things which are not convenient;

Genesis 12:1–3

Now the LORD had said unto Abram, Get thee out of thy country, and from thy kindred, and from thy father's house, unto a land that I will shew thee:

And I will make of thee a great nation, and I will bless thee, and make thy name great; and thou shalt be a blessing:

And I will bless them that bless thee, and curse him that curseth thee: and in thee shall all families of the earth be blessed.

Genesis 18:18

Seeing that Abraham shall surely become a great and mighty nation, and all the nations of the earth shall be blessed in him?

Genesis 15:18

In the same day the LORD made a covenant with Abram, saying, Unto thy seed have I given this land, from the river of Egypt unto the great river, the river Euphrates:

The Kenites, and the Kenizzites, and the Kadmonites,

And the Hittites, and the Perizzites, and the Rephaims,

And the Amorites, and the Canaanites, and the Girgashites, and the Jebusites.

Genesis 17:8

And I will give unto thee, and to thy seed after thee, the land wherein thou art a stranger, all the land of Canaan, for an everlasting possession; and I will be their God.

ISRAEL—GOD'S CHOSEN NATION ON EARTH THE MIDDLE WALL OF PARTITION ERECTED

G od had promised to make a great nation from Abraham's seed, but there was a problem. Abraham and his wife Sarah did not have any children.

They were getting older and older. Eventually they were too old to have children. This is when God gave them a miracle child, Isaac. The Abrahamic covenant was passed on to him[28] and then to his son, Jacob.[29]

God changed Jacob's name to Israel, which means "Prince of God." Israel had twelve sons. They became the twelve tribes of Israel. The Abrahamic covenant was passed to them.[30]

From this point forward, God's nation would be named Israel. People of all other nations were Gentiles. God made a difference between Israel and the Gentiles and erected what He called "the middle wall of partition" between them.[31]

---

[28] Genesis 17:19, 21.
[29] Genesis 28:13–14.
[30] Psalm 105:8–11.
[31] Leviticus 20:24; Ephesians 2:11, 14.

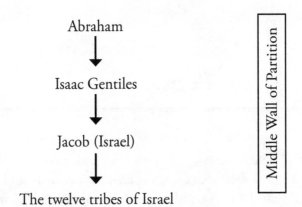

Abraham

Isaac Gentiles

Jacob (Israel)

The twelve tribes of Israel

Middle Wall of Partition

Scripture Verses

Genesis 17:19, 21

And God said, Sarah thy wife shall bear thee a son indeed; and thou shalt call his name Isaac: and I will establish my covenant with him for an everlasting covenant, and with his seed after him.

And as for Ishmael, I have heard thee: Behold, I have blessed him, and will make him fruitful, and will multiply him exceedingly; twelve princes shall he beget, and I will make him a great nation.

But my covenant will I establish with Isaac, which Sarah shall bear unto thee at this set time in the next year.

Genesis 28:13–14

And, behold, the LORD stood above it, and said, I am the LORD God of Abraham thy father, and the God of Isaac: the land whereon thou liest, to thee will I give it, and to thy seed;

And thy seed shall be as the dust of the earth, and thou shalt spread abroad to the west, and to the east, and to the north, and to the south: and in thee and in thy seed shall all the families of the earth be blessed.

Psalm 105:8–11

He hath remembered his covenant for ever, the word which he commanded to a thousand generations.

Which covenant he made with Abraham, and his oath unto Isaac;

And confirmed the same unto Jacob for a law, and to Israel for an everlasting covenant:

Saying, Unto thee will I give the land of Canaan, the lot of your inheritance.

Leviticus 20:24

But I have said unto you, Ye shall inherit their land, and I will give it unto you to possess it, a land that floweth with milk and honey: I am the LORD your God, which have separated you from other people.

Ephesians 2:11, 14

Wherefore remember, that ye being in time past Gentiles in the flesh, who are called Uncircumcision by that which is called the Circumcision in the flesh made by hands;

For he is our peace, who hath made both one, and hath broken down the middle wall of partition between us.

NOTES

MOSES—THE DELIVERER

od told Abram (Abraham) that his seed would be strangers in a land that was not their own. They would be afflicted for four hundred years. Afterward, God would deliver them out of bondage.[32] This is indeed what happened.

The sons of Jacob (Israel) became slaves in Egypt. But just as God had promised, after four hundred years, He sent a deliverer, Moses, to take His people out of Egypt to their promised land. Through Moses God worked many great signs and wonders that proved that the earth belonged to Him and that the children of Israel were His people. God defeated the gods of the Egyptians,[33] destroyed Pharaoh and his army in the Red Sea, and brought Israel safely out of Egypt.

He said that Israel would "be a peculiar treasure unto me above all people: **for all the earth is mine**."[34]

God's people had gone down to Egypt as a small family, but by the time they exited Egypt, they were over a million in number. Their passage through the Red Sea, out of Egypt, was their birth as a nation. God called them His "son" and His "firstborn."[35]

---

[32] Genesis 15:13–16.
[33] Exodus 12:12.
[34] Exodus 19:5–6.
[35] Exodus 4:22, Numbers 11:11–12.

Scripture Verses

Genesis 15:13–15

Then He said to Abram: "Know certainly that your descendants will be strangers in a land that *is* not theirs, and will serve them, and they will afflict them four hundred years. And also the nation whom they serve I will judge; afterward they shall come out with great possessions. Now as for you, you shall go to your fathers in peace; you shall be buried at a good old age."

Exodus 12:12

For I will pass through the land of Egypt on that night, and will strike all the firstborn in the land of Egypt, both man and beast; and against all the gods of Egypt I will execute judgment: I *am* the Lord.

Exodus 19:5–6

"Now therefore, if you will indeed obey My voice and keep My covenant, then you shall be a special treasure to Me above all people; for all the earth *is* Mine. And you shall be to Me a kingdom of priests and a holy nation." These *are* the words which you shall speak to the children of Israel.

Exodus 4:22

Then you shall say to Pharaoh, "Thus says the Lord: 'Israel *is* My son, My firstborn.'"

Numbers 11:11–12

So Moses said to the Lord, "Why have You afflicted Your servant? And why have I not found favor in Your sight, that You have laid the burden of all these people on me? Did I conceive all these people? Did I beget them, that You should say to me, 'Carry them in your bosom, as a guardian carries a nursing child,' to the land which You swore to their fathers?"

NOTES

The Mosaic Covenant
Israel to Be a Kingdom of Priests

When Israel left Egypt, God was with them. He said, "Ye have seen...*how* I bare you on eagles' wings, and brought you unto myself."[36] In the wilderness, He miraculously provided for all their needs. He sent manna (bread from heaven), quail, and water. Their clothes and their shoes did not wear out.[37]

God was with them every step of the way, yet the people constantly murmured and lost trust in God. Because of this, it took forty years for them to enter into their promised land. (The generation of those who doubted God had to die before the rest could enter in.)[38]

Through Moses, God gave the people of Israel His law, statutes, and judgments.

The purpose of this was to set them apart from all the other people.[39] They were supposed to be a light and an example to the rest of the nations.[40]

The law was a conditional system of blessing. Under the law, God said that if Israel obeyed, He would bless them in their land and make them a kingdom of priests and a holy nation;[41] however, if they

---

36 Exodus 19:4.
37 Exodus 16:12–15, 15:24–25, 1:6, 4:22; Deuteronomy 29:5.
38 Numbers 14:22–23, 28–35.
39 Leviticus 20:24–26.
40 Deuteronomy 4:6–8, Psalm 14:19–20.
41 Exodus 19:5–, Isaiah 61:6.

disobeyed, God would curse them. He would take them out of their land and scatter them among the nations,[42] which, we shall see, is exactly what eventually happened.

---

[42] Leviticus 26:2–33.

Scripture Verses

Exodus 19:4

You have seen what I did to the Egyptians, and how I bore you on eagles' wings and brought you to Myself.

Exodus 16:12–15

I have heard the complaints of the children of Israel. Speak to them, saying, "At twilight you shall eat meat, and in the morning you shall be filled with bread. And you shall know that I *am* the LORD your God."

So it was that quail came up at evening and covered the camp, and in the morning the dew lay all around the camp. And when the layer of dew lifted, there, on the surface of the wilderness, was a small round substance, as fine as frost on the ground. So when the children of Israel saw it, they said to one another, "What is it?" For they did not know what it was.

And Moses said to them, "This *is* the bread which the LORD has given you to eat."

Exodus 15:24–25

And the people complained against Moses, saying, "What shall we drink?" So he cried out to the LORD, and the LORD showed him a tree. When he cast it into the waters, the waters were made sweet.

Exodus 4:22

Then you shall say to Pharaoh, "Thus says the LORD: 'Israel *is* My son, My firstborn.'"

Exodus 17:6

"Behold, I will stand before you there on the rock in Horeb; and you shall strike the rock, and water will come out of it, that the people may drink."

And Moses did so in the sight of the elders of Israel.

Deuteronomy 29:5

And I have led you forty years in the wilderness. Your clothes have not worn out on you, and your sandals have not worn out on your feet.

Numbers 14:22–23

Because all these men who have seen My glory and the signs which I did in Egypt and in the wilderness, and have put Me to the test now these ten times, and have not heeded My voice, they certainly shall not see the land of which I swore to their fathers, nor shall any of those who rejected Me see it.

Numbers 14:28–35

Say to them, "As I live," says the LORD, "just as you have spoken in My hearing, so I will do to you: The carcasses of you who have complained against Me shall fall in this wilderness, all of you who were numbered, according to your entire number, from twenty years old and above. Except for Caleb the son of Jephunneh and Joshua the son of Nun, you shall by no means enter the land which I swore I would make you dwell in. But your little ones, whom you said would be victims, I will bring in, and they shall know the land which you have despised. But as for you, your carcasses shall fall in this wilderness.

"And your sons shall be shepherds in the wilderness forty years, and bear the brunt of your infidelity, until your carcasses are consumed in the wilderness. According to the number of the days in which you spied out the land, forty days, for each day you shall bear your guilt one year, namely forty years, and you shall know My rejection. I the LORD have spoken this. I will surely do so to all this evil congregation who are gathered together against Me. In this wilderness they shall be consumed, and there they shall die."

Leviticus 20:24–26

But I have said to you, "You shall inherit their land, and I will give it to you to possess, a land flowing with milk and honey." I *am* the LORD your God, who has separated you from the peoples. You shall therefore distinguish between clean animals and unclean, between unclean birds and clean, and you shall not make yourselves abominable by beast or by bird, or by any kind of living thing that creeps on the ground, which I have separated from you as unclean. And you shall be holy to Me, for I the LORD *am* holy, and have separated you from the peoples, that you should be Mine.

Deuteronomy 4:6–8

Therefore be careful to observe *them*; for this is your wisdom and your understanding in the sight of the peoples who will hear all these statutes, and say, "Surely this great nation *is* a wise and understanding people."

For what great nation is there that has God so near to it, as the LORD our God is to us, for whatever reason we may call upon Him? And what great nation *is there* that has *such* statutes and righteous judgments as are in all this law which I set before you this day?

Psalm 147:19–20

He declares His word to Jacob,

His statutes and His judgments to Israel. He has not dealt thus with any nation;

And as for *His* judgments, they have not known them.

Praise the LORD!

Exodus 19:5–6

"Now therefore, if you will indeed obey My voice and keep My covenant, then you shall be a special treasure to Me above all people; for all the earth is Mine. And you shall be to Me a kingdom of priests and a holy nation." These are the words which you shall speak to the children of Israel.

Isaiah 61:6

But you shall be named the priests of the LORD,

They shall call you the servants of our God.

You shall eat the riches of the Gentiles, And in their glory you shall boast.

Leviticus 26:27–33

And after all this, if you do not obey Me, but walk contrary to Me, then I also will walk contrary to you in fury; and I, even I, will chastise you seven times for your sins.

You shall eat the flesh of your sons, and you shall eat the flesh of your daughters.

I will destroy your high places, cut down your incense altars, and cast your carcasses on the lifeless forms of your idols; and My soul shall abhor you. I will lay your cities waste and bring your sanctuaries to desolation, and I will not smell the fragrance of your sweet aromas.

I will bring the land to desolation, and your enemies who dwell in it shall be astonished at it.

I will scatter you among the nations and draw out a sword after you; your land shall be desolate and your cities waste.

NOTES

SACRIFICES AND FEASTS OF THE LAW
A PICTURE OF ISRAEL'S REDEMPTION

B ecause all men are sinful, no one, not even God's people, could keep the law perfectly. So God gave them a means whereby they could maintain their relationship with Him. He instructed them to offer animal sacrifices as an atonement for their sins.[43]

When they believed God and offered a sacrifice *by faith*, the blood of the animals *covered* their sins. Though they did not know it, these sacrifices were a picture of the coming sacrifice of Christ that God looked forward to—the sacrifice that would *completely take away* their sins forever.[44]

Under the law, God also gave Israel feast days to observe. Three times a year all Israelite men were to go before the Lord to keep these feasts:[45]

- Unleavened bread (with Passover and firstfruits)[46]
- Feast of Harvest (also called Pentecost. It was fifty days later)[47]

---

[43] Leviticus 1:1–4.
[44] Romans 3:25, Hebrews 9:24–10:18.
[45] Exodus 23:14–17.
[46] Exodus 23:15, Leviticus 23:1–14.
[47] Exodus 23:16.

- Feast of Ingathering (trumpets, Day of Atonement, tabernacles)[48]

These feasts pictured how God would eventually redeem His people and bring them into their Promised Land and eternal kingdom. They picture real events that we will read about later.[49]

---

[48] Leviticus 23:23–44.
[49] Colossians 2:16–17.

Scripture Verses

Leviticus 1:1–4

And the LORD called unto Moses, and spake unto him out of the tabernacle of the congregation, saying,

Speak unto the children of Israel, and say unto them, If any man of you bring an offering unto the LORD, ye shall bring your offering of the cattle, even of the herd, and of the flock.

If his offering be a burnt sacrifice of the herd, let him offer a male without blemish: he shall offer it of his own voluntary will at the door of the tabernacle of the congregation before the LORD.

And he shall put his hand upon the head of the burnt offering; and it shall be accepted for him to make atonement for him.

Romans 3:25

Whom God hath set forth to be a propitiation through faith in his blood, to declare his righteousness for the remission of sins that are past, through the forbearance of God.

Hebrews 9:24–10:18

For Christ is not entered into the holy places made with hands, which are the figures of the true; but into heaven itself, now to appear in the presence of God for us:

Now where remission of these is, there is no more offering for sin.

Exodus 23:14–17

Three times thou shalt keep a feast unto me in the year.

Thou shalt keep the feast of unleavened bread: (thou shalt eat unleavened bread seven days, as I commanded thee, in the time appointed of the month Abib; for in it thou camest out from Egypt: and none shall appear before me empty:)

And the feast of harvest, the firstfruits of thy labours, which thou hast sown in the field: and the feast of ingathering, which is in the end of the year, when thou hast gathered in thy labours out of the field.

Three times in the year all thy males shall appear before the LORD God.

Exodus 23:15

Thou shalt keep the feast of unleavened bread: (thou shalt eat unleavened bread seven days, as I commanded thee, in the time appointed of the month Abib; for in it thou camest out from Egypt: and none shall appear before me empty).

Leviticus 23:1–14

And the LORD spake unto Moses, saying,

Speak unto the children of Israel, and say unto them, Concerning the feasts of the LORD, which ye shall proclaim to be holy convocations, even these are my feasts.

Six days shall work be done: but the seventh day is the sabbath of rest, an holy convocation; ye shall do no work therein: it is the sabbath of the LORD in all your dwellings.

These are the feasts of the LORD, even holy convocations, which ye shall proclaim in their seasons.

In the fourteenth day of the first month at even is the LORD's passover.

And on the fifteenth day of the same month is the feast of unleavened bread unto the LORD: seven days ye must eat unleavened bread.

In the first day ye shall have an holy convocation: ye shall do no servile work therein.

But ye shall offer an offering made by fire unto the LORD seven days: in the seventh day is an holy convocation: ye shall do no servile work therein.

And the LORD spake unto Moses, saying,

Speak unto the children of Israel, and say unto them, When ye be come into the land which I give unto you, and shall reap the harvest thereof, then ye shall bring a sheaf of the firstfruits of your harvest unto the priest:

And he shall wave the sheaf before the LORD, to be accepted for you: on the morrow after the sabbath the priest shall wave it.

And ye shall offer that day when ye wave the sheaf an he lamb without blemish of the first year for a burnt offering unto the LORD.

And the meat offering thereof shall be two tenth deals of fine flour mingled with oil, an offering made by fire unto the LORD for a sweet savour: and the drink offering thereof shall be of wine, the fourth part of an hin.

And ye shall eat neither bread, nor parched corn, nor green ears, until the selfsame day that ye have brought an offering unto your God: it shall be a statute for ever throughout your generations in all your dwellings.

Exodus 23:16

And the feast of harvest, the firstfruits of thy labours, which thou hast sown in the field: and the feast of ingathering, which is in the end of the year, when thou hast gathered in thy labours out of the field.

Leviticus 23:23–44

And the LORD spake unto Moses, saying,

Speak unto the children of Israel, saying, In the seventh month, in the first day of the month, shall ye have a sabbath, a memorial of blowing of trumpets, an holy convocation.

Ye shall do no servile work therein: but ye shall offer an offering made by fire unto the LORD.

And the LORD spake unto Moses, saying,

Also on the tenth day of this seventh month there shall be a day of atonement: it shall be an holy convocation unto you; and ye shall afflict your souls, and offer an offering made by fire unto the LORD.

And ye shall do no work in that same day: for it is a day of atonement, to make an atonement for you before the LORD your God.

For whatsoever soul it be that shall not be afflicted in that same day, he shall be cut off from among his people.

And whatsoever soul it be that doeth any work in that same day, the same soul will I destroy from among his people.

Ye shall do no manner of work: it shall be a statute for ever throughout your generations in all your dwellings.

It shall be unto you a sabbath of rest, and ye shall afflict your souls: in the ninth day of the month at even, from even unto even, shall ye celebrate your sabbath.

And the LORD spake unto Moses, saying,

Speak unto the children of Israel, saying, The fifteenth day of this seventh month shall be the feast of tabernacles for seven days unto the LORD.

On the first day shall be an holy convocation: ye shall do no servile work therein.

Seven days ye shall offer an offering made by fire unto the LORD: on the eighth day shall be an holy convocation unto you; and ye shall offer an offering made by fire unto the LORD: it is a solemn assembly; and ye shall do no servile work therein.

These are the feasts of the LORD, which ye shall proclaim to be holy convocations, to offer an offering made by fire unto the LORD, a burnt offering, and a meat offering, a sacrifice, and drink offerings, every thing upon his day:

Beside the sabbaths of the LORD, and beside your gifts, and beside all your vows, and beside all your freewill offerings, which ye give unto the LORD.

Also in the fifteenth day of the seventh month, when ye have gathered in the fruit of the land, ye shall keep a feast unto the LORD seven days: on the first day shall be a sabbath, and on the eighth day shall be a sabbath.

And ye shall take you on the first day the boughs of goodly trees, branches of palm trees, and the boughs of thick trees, and willows of the brook; and ye shall rejoice before the LORD your God seven days.

And ye shall keep it a feast unto the LORD seven days in the year. It shall be a statute for ever in your generations: ye shall celebrate it in the seventh month.

Ye shall dwell in booths seven days; all that are Israelites born shall dwell in booths: That your generations may know that I made the children of Israel to dwell in booths, when I brought them out of the land of Egypt: I am the LORD your God.

And Moses declared unto the children of Israel the feasts of the LORD.

Colossians 2:16–17

Let no man therefore judge you in meat, or in drink, or in respect of an holyday, or of the new moon, or of the sabbath days:

Which are a shadow of things to come; but the body is of Christ.

NOTES

THE DAVIDIC COVENANT
A THRONE AND KINGDOM
ON EARTH FOREVER

T hen Israel first entered their promised land, they went through periods of obedience and disobedience. Eventually, though, a great king arose who served God. His name was David. Under David, Israel had a mighty kingdom, and God made a special promise to him.

To David, God revealed a little more about His plan to regain the earth. He promised that one day David's seed, who will also be *God's son*, will sit on *David's throne in Jerusalem and rule over Israel forever*. Once that happens, Israel will dwell in the *land* promised to Abraham *forever*, and God's kingdom will be established on the earth *forever*.[50]

It is important to recognize that the kingdom described in the Davidic covenant is a literal, physical kingdom to be established upon this earth, just like David's kingdom.

---

[50]   2 Samuel 7:10–17.

Scripture Verses

2 Samuel 7:10–17

Moreover I will appoint a place for my people Israel, and will plant them, that they may dwell in a place of their own, and move no more; neither shall the children of wickedness afflict them any more, as beforetime,

And as since the time that I commanded judges to be over my people Israel, and have caused thee to rest from all thine enemies. Also the LORD telleth thee that he will make thee an house.

And when thy days be fulfilled, and thou shalt sleep with thy fathers, I will set up thy seed after thee, which shall proceed out of thy bowels, and I will establish his kingdom.

He shall build an house for my name, and I will stablish the throne of his kingdom for ever.

I will be his father, and he shall be my son. If he commit iniquity, I will chasten him with the rod of men, and with the stripes of the children of men:

But my mercy shall not depart away from him, as I took it from Saul, whom I put away before thee.

And thine house and thy kingdom shall be established for ever before thee: thy throne shall be established for ever.

According to all these words, and according to all this vision, so did Nathan speak unto David.

NOTES

ISRAEL SCATTERED

David's son Solomon ruled next. His kingdom was a magnificent kingdom. At the height of its glory, it was a picture and type of the kingdom reign of God's son, the Lord Jesus Christ. The entire world heard of its glory, and kings and queens came to see it and honor Solomon.[51]

For most of Solomon's reign, he served God. However, in his later years, he took many wives who led him into idolatry. Because of this, Israel's kingdom was split into two parts: Israel (ten tribes) and Judah (two tribes).[52]

Then, every king in Israel (the northern kingdom, also called Samaria) led the people into idolatry. So as God had warned under the law, He took them out of the land by letting the Assyrians conquer them and carry them away.[53] Later, Judah (the southern kingdom) also went into idolatry and was taken out of their land by the Babylonians.

The people of Israel were now scattered among the Gentiles, out of their land.

This was God's judgment upon them.

---

[51]   1 Kings 10:23–25.
[52]   1 Kings 11:9–13, 31–39.
[53]   2 Kings 17:6–41.

Scripture Verses

1 Kings 10:23–25

So king Solomon exceeded all the kings of the earth for riches and for wisdom.

And all the earth sought to Solomon, to hear his wisdom, which God had put in his heart.

And they brought every man his present, vessels of silver, and vessels of gold, and garments, and armour, and spices, horses, and mules, a rate year by year.

1 Kings 11:9–13

And the LORD was angry with Solomon, because his heart was turned from the LORD God of Israel, which had appeared unto him twice,

And had commanded him concerning this thing, that he should not go after other gods: but he kept not that which the LORD commanded.

Wherefore the LORD said unto Solomon, Forasmuch as this is done of thee, and thou hast not kept my covenant and my statutes, which I have commanded thee, I will surely rend the kingdom from thee, and will give it to thy servant.

Notwithstanding in thy days I will not do it for David thy father's sake: but I will rend it out of the hand of thy son.

Howbeit I will not rend away all the kingdom; but will give one tribe to thy son for David my servant's sake, and for Jerusalem's sake which I have chosen.

1 Kings 11:31–39

And he said to Jeroboam, Take thee ten pieces: for thus saith the LORD, the God of Israel, Behold, I will rend the kingdom out of the hand of Solomon, and will give ten tribes to thee:

(But he shall have one tribe for my servant David's sake, and for Jerusalem's sake, the city which I have chosen out of all the tribes of Israel.)

Because that they have forsaken me, and have worshipped Ashtoreth the goddess of the Zidonians, Chemosh the god of the Moabites, and Milcom the god of the children of Ammon, and have not walked in my ways, to do that which is right in mine eyes, and to keep my statutes and my judgments, as did David his father.

Howbeit I will not take the whole kingdom out of his hand: but I will make him prince all the days of his life for David my servant's sake, whom I chose, because he kept my commandments and my statutes:

But I will take the kingdom out of his son's hand, and will give it unto thee, even ten tribes.

And unto his son will I give one tribe, that David my servant may have a light alway before me in Jerusalem, the city which I have chosen me to put my name there.

And I will take thee, and thou shalt reign according to all that thy soul desireth, and shalt be king over Israel.

And it shall be, if thou wilt hearken unto all that I command thee, and wilt walk in my ways, and do that is right in my sight, to keep my statutes and my commandments, as David my servant did; that I will be with thee, and build thee a sure house, as I built for David, and will give Israel unto thee.

And I will for this afflict the seed of David, but not for ever.

2 Kings 17:6–41

In the ninth year of Hoshea the king of Assyria took Samaria, and carried Israel away into Assyria, and placed them in Halah and in Habor by the river of Gozan, and in the cities of the Medes.

For so it was, that the children of Israel had sinned against the LORD their God, which had brought them up out of the land of Egypt, from under the hand of Pharaoh king of Egypt, and had feared other gods,

And walked in the statutes of the heathen, whom the LORD cast out from before the children of Israel, and of the kings of Israel, which they had made.

And the children of Israel did secretly those things that were not right against the LORD their God, and they built them high places in all their cities, from the tower of the watchmen to the fenced city.

And they set them up images and groves in every high hill, and under every green tree:

And there they burnt incense in all the high places, as did the heathen whom the LORD carried away before them; and wrought wicked things to provoke the LORD to anger:

For they served idols, whereof the LORD had said unto them, Ye shall not do this thing.

Yet the LORD testified against Israel, and against Judah, by all the prophets, and by all the seers, saying, Turn ye from your evil ways, and keep my commandments and my statutes, according to all the law which I commanded your fathers, and which I sent to you by my servants the prophets.

Notwithstanding they would not hear, but hardened their necks, like to the neck of their fathers, that did not believe in the LORD their God.

And they rejected his statutes, and his covenant that he made with their fathers, and his testimonies which he testified against them; and they followed vanity, and became vain, and went after the heathen that were round about them, concerning whom the LORD had charged them, that they should not do like them.

And they left all the commandments of the LORD their God, and made them molten images, even two calves, and made a grove, and worshipped all the host of heaven, and served Baal.

And they caused their sons and their daughters to pass through the fire, and used divination and enchantments, and sold themselves to do evil in the sight of the LORD, to provoke him to anger.

Therefore the LORD was very angry with Israel, and removed them out of his sight: there was none left but the tribe of Judah only.

Also Judah kept not the commandments of the LORD their God, but walked in the statutes of Israel which they made.

And the LORD rejected all the seed of Israel, and afflicted them, and delivered them into the hand of spoilers, until he had cast them out of his sight.

For he rent Israel from the house of David; and they made Jeroboam the son of Nebat king: and Jeroboam drave Israel from following the LORD, and made them sin a great sin.

For the children of Israel walked in all the sins of Jeroboam which he did; they departed not from them;

Until the LORD removed Israel out of his sight, as he had said by all his servants the prophets. So was Israel carried away out of their own land to Assyria unto this day.

And the king of Assyria brought men from Babylon, and from Cuthah, and from Ava, and from Hamath, and from Sepharvaim, and placed them in the cities of Samaria instead of the children of Israel: and they possessed Samaria, and dwelt in the cities thereof.

And so it was at the beginning of their dwelling there, that they feared not the LORD: therefore the LORD sent lions among them, which slew some of them.

Wherefore they spake to the king of Assyria, saying, The nations which thou hast removed, and placed in the cities of Samaria, know not the manner of the God of the land: therefore he hath sent lions among them, and, behold, they slay them, because they know not the manner of the God of the land.

Then the king of Assyria commanded, saying, Carry thither one of the priests whom ye brought from thence; and let them go and dwell there, and let him teach them the manner of the God of the land.

Then one of the priests whom they had carried away from Samaria came and dwelt in Bethel, and taught them how they should fear the LORD.

Howbeit every nation made gods of their own, and put them in the houses of the high places which the Samaritans had made, every nation in their cities wherein they dwelt.

And the men of Babylon made Succothbenoth, and the men of Cuth made Nergal, and the men of Hamath made Ashima,

And the Avites made Nibhaz and Tartak, and the Sepharvites burnt their children in fire to Adrammelech and Anammelech, the gods of Sepharvaim.

So they feared the LORD, and made unto themselves of the

lowest of them priests of the high places, which sacrificed for them in the houses of the high places.

They feared the LORD, and served their own gods, after the manner of the nations whom they carried away from thence.

Unto this day they do after the former manners: they fear not the LORD, neither do they after their statutes, or after their ordinances, or after the law and commandment which the LORD commanded the children of Jacob, whom he named Israel;

With whom the LORD had made a covenant, and charged them, saying, Ye shall not fear other gods, nor bow yourselves to them, nor serve them, nor sacrifice to them:

But the LORD, who brought you up out of the land of Egypt with great power and a stretched out arm, him shall ye fear, and him shall ye worship, and to him shall ye do sacrifice.

And the statutes, and the ordinances, and the law, and the commandment, which he wrote for you, ye shall observe to do for evermore; and ye shall not fear other gods.

And the covenant that I have made with you ye shall not forget; neither shall ye fear other gods.

But the LORD your God ye shall fear; and he shall deliver you out of the hand of all your enemies.

Howbeit they did not hearken, but they did after their former manner.

So these nations feared the LORD, and served their graven images, both their children, and their children's children: as did their fathers, so do they unto this day.

A New Covenant with Israel
God Will Put the Law
in Their Hearts

I srael had failed under the Mosaic covenant, but God would not forget His promises to Abraham, Isaac, Jacob, and David, which were not dependent upon Israel's obedience.

Through the prophets, God revealed that He will one day "make a new covenant with the house of Israel, and with the house of Judah."[54] Under the new covenant, He will do in them what they could not do on their own. God said, "I will put my law in their inward parts, and write it in their hearts." He promised,

> A new heart also will I give you [Israel]...
> And I will...cause you to walk in My statutes,
> and ye shall keep My judgments and do *them*.
> And ye shall dwell in the land that I gave to your
> fathers; and ye shall be My people, and I will be
> your God.[55]

God will one day gather Israelites from everywhere He has scattered them and bring them back into their promised land where they will dwell forever.[56] David's son, who will also be God's son, will be

---

[54] Jeremiah 31:31.
[55] Ezekiel 36:26–28.
[56] Ezekiel 37:21–28, Isaiah 11:10–12.

king over them and rule from Jerusalem in a kingdom of perfect righteousness.[57]

Israel will be the light to the Gentiles that God intended them to be—a kingdom of priests. They will bring God's salvation to the world.[58]

---

[57] Jeremiah 23:3–8, Ezekiel 37:24–28, Jeremiah 33:15–17.
[58] Isaiah 61:6–9; Isaiah 60:3–5 and 10–16; Zechariah 8:23.

Scripture Verses

Jeremiah 31:31–34

Behold, the days come, saith the LORD, that I will make a new covenant with the house of Israel, and with the house of Judah: Not according to the covenant that I made with their fathers in the day that I took them by the hand to bring them out of the land of Egypt; which my covenant they brake, although I was an husband unto them, saith the LORD:

But this shall be the covenant that I will make with the house of Israel; After those days, saith the LORD, I will put my law in their inward parts, and write it in their hearts; and will be their God, and they shall be my people.

And they shall teach no more every man his neighbour, and every man his brother, saying, Know the LORD: for they shall all know me, from the least of them unto the greatest of them, saith the LORD: for I will forgive their iniquity, and I will remember their sin no more.

Ezekiel 36:26–28

A new heart also will I give you, and a new spirit will I put within you: and I will take away the stony heart out of your flesh, and I will give you an heart of flesh.

And I will put my spirit within you, and cause you to walk in my statutes, and ye shall keep my judgments, and do them.

And ye shall dwell in the land that I gave to your fathers; and ye shall be my people, and I will be your God.

Ezekiel 37:21–28

And say unto them, Thus saith the Lord GOD; Behold, I will take the children of Israel from among the heathen, whither they be gone, and will gather them on every side, and bring them into their own land:

And I will make them one nation in the land upon the mountains of Israel; and one king shall be king to them all: and they shall be no more two nations, neither shall they be divided into two kingdoms any more at all.

Neither shall they defile themselves any more with their idols, nor with their detestable things, nor with any of their transgressions: but I will save them out of all their dwellingplaces, wherein they have sinned, and will cleanse them: so shall they be my people, and I will be their God.

And David my servant shall be king over them; and they all shall have one shepherd: they shall also walk in my judgments, and observe my statutes, and do them.

And they shall dwell in the land that I have given unto Jacob my servant, wherein your fathers have dwelt; and they shall dwell therein, even they, and their children, and their children's children for ever: and my servant David shall be their prince for ever.

Moreover I will make a covenant of peace with them; it shall be an everlasting covenant with them: and I will place them, and multiply them, and will set my sanctuary in the midst of them for evermore.

My tabernacle also shall be with them: yea, I will be their God, and they shall be my people.

And the heathen shall know that I the LORD do sanctify Israel, when my sanctuary shall be in the midst of them for evermore.

Isaiah 11:10–12

And in that day there shall be a root of Jesse, which shall stand for an ensign of the people; to it shall the Gentiles seek: and his rest shall be glorious.

And it shall come to pass in that day, that the Lord shall set his hand again the second time to recover the remnant of his people, which shall be left, from Assyria, and from Egypt, and from Pathros, and from Cush, and from Elam, and from Shinar, and from Hamath, and from the islands of the sea.

And he shall set up an ensign for the nations, and shall assemble the outcasts of Israel, and gather together the dispersed of Judah from the four corners of the earth.

Jeremiah 23:3–8

And I will gather the remnant of my flock out of all countries whither I have driven them, and will bring them again to their folds; and they shall be fruitful and increase.

And I will set up shepherds over them which shall feed them: and they shall fear no more, nor be dismayed, neither shall they be lacking, saith the LORD.

Behold, the days come, saith the LORD, that I will raise unto David a righteous Branch, and a King shall reign and prosper, and shall execute judgment and justice in the earth.

In his days Judah shall be saved, and Israel shall dwell safely: and this is his name whereby he shall be called, THE LORD OUR RIGHTEOUSNESS.

Therefore, behold, the days come, saith the LORD, that they shall no more say, The LORD liveth, which brought up the children of Israel out of the land of Egypt;

But, The LORD liveth, which brought up and which led the seed of the house of Israel out of the north country, and from all countries whither I had driven them; and they shall dwell in their own land.

Ezekiel 37:24–28

And David my servant shall be king over them; and they all shall have one shepherd: they shall also walk in my judgments, and observe my statutes, and do them.

And they shall dwell in the land that I have given unto Jacob my servant, wherein your fathers have dwelt; and they shall dwell therein, even they, and their children, and their children's children for ever: and my servant David shall be their prince for ever.

Moreover I will make a covenant of peace with them; it shall be an everlasting covenant with them: and I will place them, and multiply them, and will set my sanctuary in the midst of them for evermore.

My tabernacle also shall be with them: yea, I will be their God, and they shall be my people.

And the heathen shall know that I the LORD do sanctify Israel, when my sanctuary shall be in the midst of them for evermore.

Jeremiah 33:15–17

In those days, and at that time, will I cause the Branch of righteousness to grow up unto David; and he shall execute judgment and righteousness in the land.

In those days shall Judah be saved, and Jerusalem shall dwell safely: and this is the name wherewith she shall be called, The LORD our righteousness.

For thus saith the LORD; David shall never want a man to sit upon the throne of the house of Israel;

Isaiah 61:6–9

But ye shall be named the Priests of the LORD: men shall call you the Ministers of our God: ye shall eat the riches of the Gentiles, and in their glory shall ye boast yourselves.

For your shame ye shall have double; and for confusion they shall rejoice in their portion: therefore in their land they shall possess the double: everlasting joy shall be unto them.

For I the LORD love judgment, I hate robbery for burnt offering; and I will direct their work in truth, and I will make an everlasting covenant with them.

And their seed shall be known among the Gentiles, and their offspring among the people: all that see them shall acknowledge them, that they are the seed which the LORD hath blessed.

Isaiah 60:3-5

And the Gentiles shall come to thy light, and kings to the brightness of thy rising.

Lift up thine eyes round about, and see: all they gather themselves together, they come to thee: thy sons shall come from far, and thy daughters shall be nursed at thy side.

Then thou shalt see, and flow together, and thine heart shall fear, and be enlarged; because the abundance of the sea shall be converted unto thee, the forces of the Gentiles shall come unto thee.

Isaiah 60:10-16

And the sons of strangers shall build up thy walls, and their kings shall minister unto thee: for in my wrath I smote thee, but in my favour have I had mercy on thee.

Therefore thy gates shall be open continually; they shall not be shut day nor night; that men may bring unto thee the forces of the Gentiles, and that their kings may be brought.

For the nation and kingdom that will not serve thee shall perish; yea, those nations shall be utterly wasted.

The glory of Lebanon shall come unto thee, the fir tree, the pine tree, and the box together, to beautify the place of my sanctuary; and I will make the place of my feet glorious.

The sons also of them that afflicted thee shall come bending unto thee; and all they that despised thee shall bow themselves down at the soles of thy feet; and they shall call thee; The city of the LORD, The Zion of the Holy One of Israel.

Whereas thou has been forsaken and hated, so that no man went through thee, I will make thee an eternal excellency, a joy of many generations.

Thou shalt also suck the milk of the Gentiles, and shalt suck the breast of kings: and thou shalt know that I the LORD am thy Saviour and thy Redeemer, the mighty One of Jacob.

Zechariah 8:23

Thus saith the LORD of hosts; In those days it shall come to pass, that ten men shall take hold out of all languages of the nations, even shall take hold of the skirt of him that is a Jew, saying, We will go with you: for we have heard that God is with you.

NOTES

PROPHETS FORETELL OF ISRAEL'S KINGDOM

The prophets confirmed the promises of the new covenant and gave more details about God's plan to restore the earth to Christ's rule:

- God will send His Son to save His people (Israel) from their enemies and their sins.[59] He will conquer Satan and free His people and His land of him.[60] But He will first suffer and be "cut off" for the sins of His people (Israel).[61]
- God's Son, the seed of David, will set up His kingdom and rule the earth from Jerusalem forever.[62] The curse will be removed from the earth.[63] There will be a great healing of the people.[64]
- During the kingdom, the people of Israel will be gathered into their land where they will be a kingdom of priests and a light to the Gentiles. Nations who want to be blessed will seek God in Jerusalem and will bless Israel. (The fulfillment of the Abrahamic covenant.)[65]
- However, before the kingdom is established, God will purge Israel during a time of chastening called "the time

---

[59] Zacharias summarizes the prophets in Luke 1:67–77.
[60] Isaiah 49:24–25 with Matthew 12:29.
[61] Isaiah 53:6–12; Psalm 22; Psalm 2.
[62] Isaiah 24:23; Jeremiah 3:17; Zechariah 8:3–8; Isaiah 9:7; Jeremiah 33:15–16; Matthew 5:35.
[63] Ezekiel 36:35; Isaiah 11:6–9 and 35:1–2.
[64] Isaiah 35:5–6.
[65] Isaiah 11:10–16.

of Jacob's trouble,"[66] more commonly known as the tribulation period. He will destroy the rebels from among Israel, so that only true believers—"the little flock," "the elect," "the righteous," "the remnant"—will enter the kingdom.[67]

---

[66]   Jeremiah 30:7.
[67]   Malachi 3:2–4; Ezekiel 20:37–42.

Scripture Verses

Zacharias summarizes the prophets in Luke 1:67–77

And his father Zacharias was filled with the Holy Ghost, and prophesied, saying,

Blessed be the Lord God of Israel; for he hath visited and redeemed his people,

And hath raised up an horn of salvation for us in the house of his servant David;

As he spake by the mouth of his holy prophets, which have been since the world began:

That we should be saved from our enemies, and from the hand of all that hate us;

To perform the mercy promised to our fathers, and to remember his holy covenant;

The oath which he sware to our father Abraham,

That he would grant unto us, that we being delivered out of the hand of our enemies might serve him without fear,

In holiness and righteousness before him, all the days of our life.

And thou, child, shalt be called the prophet of the Highest: for thou shalt go before the face of the Lord to prepare his ways;

To give knowledge of salvation unto his people by the remission of their sins.

Isaiah 49:24–25

Shall the prey be taken from the mighty, or the lawful captive delivered?

But thus saith the LORD, Even the captives of the mighty shall be taken away, and the prey of the terrible shall be delivered: for I will contend with him that contendeth with thee, and I will save thy children.

Matthew 12:29

Or else how can one enter into a strong man's house, and spoil his goods, except he first bind the strong man? and then he will spoil his house.

Isaiah 53:6–12

All we like sheep have gone astray; we have turned every one to his own way; and the LORD hath laid on him the iniquity of us all.

He was oppressed, and he was afflicted, yet he opened not his mouth: he is brought as a lamb to the slaughter, and as a sheep before her shearers is dumb, so he openeth not his mouth.

He was taken from prison and from judgment: and who shall declare his generation? for he was cut off out of the land of the living: for the transgression of my people was he stricken.

And he made his grave with the wicked, and with the rich in his death; because he had done no violence, neither was any deceit in his mouth.

Yet it pleased the LORD to bruise him; he hath put him to grief: when thou shalt make his soul an offering for sin, he shall see his seed, he shall prolong his days, and the pleasure of the LORD shall prosper in his hand.

He shall see of the travail of his soul, and shall be satisfied: by his knowledge shall my righteous servant justify many; for he shall bear their iniquities.

Therefore will I divide him a portion with the great, and he shall divide the spoil with the strong; because he hath poured out his soul unto death: and he was numbered with the transgressors; and he bare the sin of many, and made intercession for the transgressors.

Psalm 22

My God, my God, why hast thou forsaken me? why art thou so far from helping me, and from the words of my roaring?

O my God, I cry in the day time, but thou hearest not; and in the night season, and am not silent.

But thou art holy, O thou that inhabitest the praises of Israel.

Our fathers trusted in thee: they trusted, and thou didst deliver them.

They cried unto thee, and were delivered: they trusted in thee, and were not confounded. 6 But I am a worm, and no man;

a reproach of men, and despised of the people.

All they that see me laugh me to scorn: they shoot out the lip, they shake the head, saying,

He trusted on the LORD that he would deliver him: let him deliver him, seeing he delighted in him.

But thou art he that took me out of the womb: thou didst make me hope when I was upon my mother's breasts.

I was cast upon thee from the womb: thou art my God from my mother's belly.

Be not far from me; for trouble is near; for there is none to help.

Many bulls have compassed me: strong bulls of Bashan have beset me round.

They gaped upon me with their mouths, as a ravening and a roaring lion.

I am poured out like water, and all my bones are out of joint: my heart is like wax; it is melted in the midst of my bowels.

My strength is dried up like a potsherd; and my tongue cleaveth to my jaws; and thou hast brought me into the dust of death.

For dogs have compassed me: the assembly of the wicked have inclosed me: they pierced my hands and my feet.

I may tell all my bones: they look and stare upon me.

They part my garments among them, and cast lots upon my vesture.

But be not thou far from me, O LORD: O my strength, haste thee to help me.

Deliver my soul from the sword; my darling from the power of the dog.

Save me from the lion's mouth: for thou hast heard me from the horns of the unicorns.

I will declare thy name unto my brethren: in the midst of the congregation will I praise thee.

Ye that fear the LORD, praise him; all ye the seed of Jacob, glorify him; and fear him, all ye the seed of Israel.

For he hath not despised nor abhorred the affliction of the afflicted; neither hath he hid his face from him; but when he cried unto him, he heard.

My praise shall be of thee in the great congregation: I will pay my vows before them that fear him.

The meek shall eat and be satisfied: they shall praise the LORD that seek him: your heart shall live for ever.

All the ends of the world shall remember and turn unto the LORD: and all the kindreds of the nations shall worship before thee.

For the kingdom is the LORD's: and he is the governor among the nations.

All they that be fat upon earth shall eat and worship: all they that go down to the dust shall bow before him: and none can keep alive his own soul.

A seed shall serve him; it shall be accounted to the Lord for a generation.

They shall come, and shall declare his righteousness unto a people that shall be born, that he hath done this.

Psalm 2

Why do the heathen rage, and the people imagine a vain thing?

The kings of the earth set themselves, and the rulers take counsel together, against the LORD, and against his anointed, saying,

Let us break their bands asunder, and cast away their cords from us.

He that sitteth in the heavens shall laugh: the LORD shall have them in derision.

Then shall he speak unto them in his wrath, and vex them in his sore displeasure.

Yet have I set my king upon my holy hill of Zion.

I will declare the decree: the LORD hath said unto me, Thou art my Son; this day have I begotten thee.

Ask of me, and I shall give thee the heathen for thine inheritance, and the uttermost parts of the earth for thy possession.

Thou shalt break them with a rod of iron; thou shalt dash them in pieces like a potter's vessel.

Be wise now therefore, O ye kings: be instructed, ye judges of the earth.

Serve the LORD with fear, and rejoice with trembling.

Kiss the Son, lest he be angry, and ye perish from the way, when his wrath is kindled but a little. Blessed are all they that put their trust in him.

Isaiah 24:23

Then the moon shall be confounded, and the sun ashamed, when the LORD of hosts shall reign in mount Zion, and in Jerusalem, and before his ancients gloriously.

Jeremiah 3:17

At that time they shall call Jerusalem the throne of the LORD; and all the nations shall be gathered unto it, to the name of the LORD, to Jerusalem: neither shall they walk any more after the imagination of their evil heart.

Zechariah 8:3–8

Thus saith the LORD; I am returned unto Zion, and will dwell in the midst of Jerusalem: and Jerusalem shall be called a city of truth; and the mountain of the LORD of hosts the holy mountain.

Thus saith the LORD of hosts; There shall yet old men and old women dwell in the streets of Jerusalem, and every man with his staff in his hand for very age.

And the streets of the city shall be full of boys and girls playing in the streets thereof.

Thus saith the LORD of hosts; If it be marvellous in the eyes of the remnant of this people in these days, should it also be marvellous in mine eyes? saith the LORD of hosts.

Thus saith the LORD of hosts; Behold, I will save my people from the east country, and from the west country;

And I will bring them, and they shall dwell in the midst of Jerusalem: and they shall be my people, and I will be their God, in truth and in righteousness.

Isaiah 9:7

Of the increase of his government and peace there shall be no end, upon the throne of David, and upon his kingdom, to order it, and to establish it with judgment and with justice from henceforth even for ever. The zeal of the LORD of hosts will perform this.

Jeremiah 33:15–16

In those days, and at that time, will I cause the Branch of righteousness to grow up unto David; and he shall execute judgment and righteousness in the land.

In those days shall Judah be saved, and Jerusalem shall dwell safely: and this is the name wherewith she shall be called, The LORD our righteousness.

Matthew 5:35

Nor by the earth; for it is his footstool: neither by Jerusalem; for it is the city of the great King.

Ezekiel 36:35

And they shall say, This land that was desolate is become like the garden of Eden; and the waste and desolate and ruined cities are become fenced, and are inhabited.

Isaiah 11:6–9

The wolf also shall dwell with the lamb, and the leopard shall lie down with the kid; and the calf and the young lion and the fatling together; and a little child shall lead them.

And the cow and the bear shall feed; their young ones shall lie down together: and the lion shall eat straw like the ox. And the sucking child shall play on the hole of the asp, and the weaned child shall put his hand on the cockatrice' den.

They shall not hurt nor destroy in all my holy mountain: for the earth shall be full of the knowledge of the LORD, as the waters cover the sea.

Isaiah 35:1–2

The wilderness and the solitary place shall be glad for them; and the desert shall rejoice, and blossom as the rose.

It shall blossom abundantly, and rejoice even with joy and singing: the glory of Lebanon shall be given unto it, the excellency of Carmel and Sharon, they shall see the glory of the LORD, and the excellency of our God.

Isaiah 35:5–6

Then the eyes of the blind shall be opened, and the ears of the deaf shall be unstopped.

Then shall the lame man leap as an hart, and the tongue of the dumb sing: for in the wilderness shall waters break out, and streams in the desert.

Isaiah 11:10–16

And in that day there shall be a Root of Jesse,

Who shall stand as a banner to the people; For the Gentiles shall seek Him,

And His resting place shall be glorious."

It shall come to pass in that day

That the Lord shall set His hand again the second time

To recover the remnant of His people who are left, From Assyria and Egypt, From Pathros and Cush, From Elam and Shinar, From Hamath and the islands of the sea.

He will set up a banner for the nations, And will assemble the outcasts of Israel, And gather together the dispersed of Judah From the four corners of the earth.

Also the envy of Ephraim shall depart, and the adversaries of Judah shall be cut off; Ephraim shall not envy Judah, and Judah shall not harass Ephraim.

But they shall fly down upon the shoulder of the Philistines toward the west;

Together they shall plunder the people of the East;

They shall lay their hand on Edom and Moab;

And the people of Ammon shall obey them.

The LORD will utterly destroy the tongue of the Sea of Egypt;

With His mighty wind He will shake His fist over the River,

And strike it in the seven streams, And make men cross over dry-shod.

There will be a highway for the remnant of His people

Who will be left from Assyria, As it was for Israel

In the day that he came up from the land of Egypt.

Jeremiah 30:7

Alas! For that day *is* great, So that none *is* like it;

And it *is* the time of Jacob's trouble, But he shall be saved out of it.

Malachi 3:2–4

But who can endure the day of His coming?

And who can stand when He appears? For He is like a refiner's fire

And like launderers' soap.

He will sit as a refiner and a purifier of silver;

He will purify the sons of Levi, And purge them as gold

and silver, That they may offer to the LORD

An offering in righteousness.

"Then the offering of Judah and Jerusalem

Will be pleasant to the LORD, As in the days of old,

As in former years.

Ezekiel 20:37–42

"I will make you pass under the rod, and I will bring you into the bond of the covenant; I will purge the rebels from among you, and those who transgress against Me; I will bring them out of the country where they dwell, but they shall not enter the land of Israel. Then you will know that I am the LORD.

As for you, O house of Israel," thus says the Lord GOD: "Go, serve every one of you his idols—and hereafter—if you will not obey Me; but profane My holy name no more with your gifts and your idols. For on My holy mountain, on the mountain height of Israel," says the Lord GOD, "there all the house of Israel, all of them in the land, shall serve Me; there I will accept them, and there I will require your offerings and the firstfruits of your sacrifices, together with all your holy things. I will accept you as a sweet aroma when I bring you out from the peoples and gather you out of the countries where you have been scattered; and I will be hallowed in you before the Gentiles. Then you shall know that I am the LORD, when I bring you into the land of Israel, into the country for which I raised My hand in an oath to give to your fathers.

NOTES

DANIEL'S TIME SCHEDULE

T he prophet Daniel gave a time schedule of the events that will occur prior to the establishment of God's kingdom— the kingdom of heaven upon the earth.[68] He prophesied that sixty-nine weeks of years (483 years) after "the commandment to restore and to build Jerusalem," Messiah would come.[69]

So once this event happened, those who believed God's Word could count the years until Messiah would come. According to Sir Robert Anderson, 483 years after the commandment was given is the very day that Christ rode into Jerusalem on the foal of a donkey.[70]

Daniel had been taken to Babylon when King Nebuchadnezzar's army invaded Judah. The king had a dream that Daniel interpreted. The dream revealed that, beginning with the Babylonian Empire, Gentile kingdoms would rule over Israel until Messiah establishes God's kingdom.[71] This era of Gentile domination is called "the times of the Gentiles."[72]

After the last Old Testament prophet wrote, God would not speak again until He would send the prophet to announce the arrival of the Messiah.

---

[68] Daniel 2:44, Deuteronomy 11:21.
[69] Daniel 9:25.
[70] Daniel 2:36–45.
[71] Luke 21:24.
[72] Amos 8:11–12.

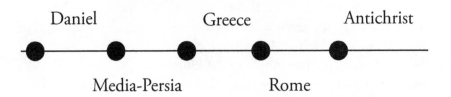

Scripture Verses

Daniel 2:44

And in the days of these kings the God of heaven will set up a kingdom which shall never be destroyed; and the kingdom shall not be left to other people; it shall break in pieces and consume all these kingdoms, and it shall stand forever.

Deuteronomy 11:21

That your days and the days of your children may be multiplied in the land of which the LORD swore to your fathers to give them, like the days of the heavens above the earth.

Daniel 9:25

Know therefore and understand, *that* from the going forth of the command to restore and build Jerusalem until Messiah the Prince, *there shall be* seven weeks and sixty-two weeks; the street shall be built again, and the wall, even in troublesome times.

Daniel 2:36–45

This is the dream. Now we will tell the interpretation of it before the king. You, O king, are a king of kings. For the God of heaven has given you a kingdom, power, strength, and glory; and wherever the children of men dwell, or the beasts of the field and the birds of the heaven, He has given them into your hand, and has made you ruler over them all—you are this head of gold. But after you shall arise another kingdom inferior to yours; then another, a third kingdom of bronze, which shall rule over all the earth. And the fourth kingdom shall be as strong as iron, inasmuch as iron breaks in pieces and shatters everything; and like iron that crushes, that kingdom will break in pieces and crush all the others. Whereas you saw the feet and toes, partly of potter's clay and partly of iron, the kingdom shall be divided;

yet the strength of the iron shall be in it, just as you saw the iron mixed with ceramic clay. And as the toes of the feet were partly of iron and partly of clay, so the kingdom shall be partly strong and partly fragile. As you saw iron mixed with ceramic clay, they will mingle with the seed of men; but they will not adhere to one another, just as iron does not mix with clay. And in the days of these kings the God of heaven will set up a kingdom which shall never be destroyed; and the kingdom shall not be left to other people; it shall break in pieces and consume all these kingdoms, and it shall stand forever. Inasmuch as you saw that the stone was cut out of the mountain without hands, and that it broke in pieces the iron, the bronze, the clay, the silver, and the gold—the great God has made known to the king what will come to pass after this. The dream is certain, and its interpretation is sure.

Luke 21:24

And they will fall by the edge of the sword, and be led away captive into all nations. And Jerusalem will be trampled by Gentiles until the times of the Gentiles are fulfilled.

Amos 8:11–12

"Behold, the days are coming," says the Lord GOD, "That I will send a famine on the land,

Not a famine of bread, Nor a thirst for water,

But of hearing the words of the LORD."

12 They shall wander from sea to sea, And from north to east;

They shall run to and fro, seeking the word of the LORD, But shall not find it.

NOTES

Gospels and Early Acts

Covenants and Prophecies Begin to Be Fulfilled

"The Time Is Fulfilled and the Kingdom of God Is at Hand"

God was silent for four hundred years. Then, right on time, Messiah was born. It is significant that Matthew begins by telling us that Jesus Christ is "the son of David, the son of Abraham" because Jesus Christ came to fulfill the Davidic and Abrahamic covenants.[73] To understand the earthly ministry of Christ, you must understand the Old Testament covenants and prophecies.

God broke His silence by sending John the Baptist—"the voice of one crying in the wilderness"[74]—to announce the arrival of the Messiah and the "at hand" phase of the kingdom God had promised Israel. John is called the greatest prophet[75] because, as Christ stated, "the law and the prophets were **until** John: since that time the kingdom of God is preached."[76] The law and the prophets before John had proclaimed that the kingdom was coming, but with the arrival of the Messiah, *John was sent to announce that the kingdom was at hand.*[77]

---

[73] Matthew 1:1–16,
Romans 15:8–9,
Romans 9:4–5.

[74] Isaiah 4:3, Matthew 3:3.

[75] Luke 7:28.

[76] Luke 16:16.

[77] Matthew 3:2, John 1:6.

Scripture Verses

Matthew 1:1

The book of the genealogy[a] of Jesus Christ, the Son of David, the Son of Abraham:

The family tree of Jesus Christ, David's son, Abraham's son:

Abraham had Isaac, Isaac had Jacob,

Jacob had Judah and his brothers,

Judah had Perez and Zerah (the mother was Tamar),

Perez had Hezron, Hezron had Aram, Aram had Amminadab,

Amminadab had Nahshon, Nahshon had Salmon,

Salmon had Boaz (his mother was Rahab), Boaz had Obed (Ruth was the mother), Obed had Jesse,

Jesse had David, and David became king.

David had Solomon (Uriah's wife was the mother),

Solomon had Rehoboam, Rehoboam had Abijah, Abijah had Asa,

Asa had Jehoshaphat, Jehoshaphat had Joram, Joram had Uzziah, Uzziah had Jotham, Jotham had Ahaz,

Ahaz had Hezekiah, Hezekiah had Manasseh, Manasseh had Amon, Amon had Josiah,

Josiah had Jehoiachin and his brothers, and then the people were taken into the Babylonian exile.

When the Babylonian exile ended, Jeconiah had Shealtiel, Shealtiel had Zerubbabel, Zerubbabel had Abiud, Abiud had Eliakim, Eliakim had Azor,

Azor had Zadok, Zadok had Achim, Achim had Eliud, Eliud had Eleazar, Eleazar had Matthan, Matthan had Jacob,

Jacob had Joseph, Mary's husband, the Mary who gave birth to Jesus, the Jesus who was called Christ.

Romans 15:8–9

Now I say that Jesus Christ has become a servant to the circumcision for the truth of God, to confirm the promises made to the fathers, and that the Gentiles might glorify God for His mercy, as it is written:

Romans 9:4–5

Who are Israelites, to whom pertain the adoption, the glory, the covenants, the giving of the law, the service of God, and the promises; of whom are the fathers and from whom, according to the flesh, Christ came, who is over all, the eternally blessed God. Amen.

Isaiah 40:3

The voice of one crying in the wilderness: "Prepare the way of the LORD;

Make straight in the desert A highway for our God."

Matthew 3:3

For this is he who was spoken of by the prophet Isaiah, saying:

"The voice of one crying in the wilderness:

'Prepare the way of the LORD; Make His paths straight.'"

Luke 7:28

For I say to you, among those born of women there is not a greater prophet than John the Baptist; but he who is least in the kingdom of God is greater than he.

Luke 16:16

The law and the prophets were until John. Since that time the kingdom of God has been preached, and everyone is pressing into it.

Matthew 3:2

And saying, "Repent, for the kingdom of heaven is at hand!"

John 1:6

There was a man sent from God, whose name was John.

NOTES

JOHN THE BAPTIST: THE FORERUNNER

As prophesied, God sent His messenger, the forerunner, John, to announce to Israel, "**Repent, for the kingdom of heaven is at hand**."[78] (It is called "the kingdom of heaven" because it is heavenly in nature. Clearly, it is the kingdom promised to Israel in the Old Testament. The "God of heaven" will establish it upon this earth [Dan. 2:44]. Deuteronomy 11:21 calls it "the days of heaven **upon the earth**.")

At that time Israel, spiritually, was ruled by the religious traditions of the scribes and Pharisees, who were Satan's pawns.[79] Satan had also filled the land and the nation with his devils because he knew it was time for God's Son to claim His land and His people. So John went outside of Jerusalem, into the wilderness, to separate himself from the apostate nation and to call out a remnant of those who would believe.[80]

Those who responded to John were baptized "*for the remission of sins*."[81] Water baptism separated them from "the generation of vipers" who will be purged out of Israel during "the wrath to come."[82] Water baptism was also necessary for Israel at that time because, under the law, water washing was required for cleansing those who would serve in the priesthood.[83] Remember, Israel was to be a "king-

---

[78] Matthew 3:2; John 1:31; Malachi 3:1.
[79] Matthew 15:3–9 and Matthew 23 (all); John 8:4.
[80] Matthew 3:1–7.
[81] Mark 1:4; Luke 3:3.
[82] Matthew 3:7; Luke 7:30; Matthew 23:35–36.
[83] Exodus 29:4.

dom of priests,"[84] God's channel of blessing to the rest of the world—but they had become unclean.

To reach the world, God had to first cleanse and save Israel

---

[84]   Exodus 19:5–6 and Isaiah 61:6–9.

Scripture Verses

Matthew 3:2

And saying, "Repent, for the kingdom of heaven is at hand!"

John 1:31

I did not know Him; but that He should be revealed to Israel, therefore I came baptizing with water.

Malachi 3:1

Behold, I send My messenger,

And he will prepare the way before Me. And the Lord, whom you seek,

Will suddenly come to His temple, Even the Messenger of the covenant, In whom you delight.

Behold, He is coming," Says the LORD of hosts.

Matthew 15:3–9

He answered and said to them, "Why do you also transgress the commandment of God because of your tradition? For God commanded, saying, 'Honor your father and your mother'; and, 'He who curses father or mother, let him be put to death.' But you say, 'Whoever says to his father or mother, "Whatever profit you might have received from me is a gift to God"—then he need not honor his father or mother.' Thus you have made the commandment of God of no effect by your tradition. Hypocrites! Well did Isaiah prophesy about you, saying:

'These people draw near to Me with their mouth, And honor Me with their lips, But their heart is far from Me. And in vain they worship Me, Teaching as doctrines the commandments of men.'"

Matthew 23

Then Jesus spoke to the multitudes and to His disciples, saying: "The scribes and the Pharisees sit in Moses' seat. Therefore whatever they tell you to observe, that observe and do, but do not do according to their works; for they say, and do not do. For they bind heavy burdens, hard to bear, and lay them on men's shoulders; but they themselves will not move them with one of their fingers.

But all their works they do to be seen by men. They make their phylacteries broad and enlarge the borders of their garments. They love the best places at feasts, the best seats in the synagogues, greetings in the marketplaces, and to be called by men, 'Rabbi, Rabbi.'

But you, do not be called 'Rabbi'; for One is your Teacher, the Christ, and you are all brethren. Do not call anyone on earth your father; for One is your Father, He who is in heaven. And do not be called teachers; for

One is your Teacher, the Christ. But he who is greatest among you shall be your servant. And whoever exalts himself will be humbled, and he who humbles himself will be exalted.

"But woe to you, scribes and Pharisees, hypocrites! For you shut up the kingdom of heaven against men; for you neither go in yourselves, nor do you allow those who are entering to go in. Woe to you, scribes and Pharisees, hypocrites! For you devour widows' houses, and for a pretense make long prayers. Therefore you will receive greater condemnation.

"Woe to you, scribes and Pharisees, hypocrites! For you travel land and sea to win one proselyte, and when he is won, you make him twice as much a son of hell as yourselves.

"Woe to you, blind guides, who say, 'Whoever swears by the temple, it is nothing; but whoever swears by the gold of the temple, he is obliged to perform it.' Fools and blind! For which is greater, the gold or the temple that sanctifies the gold? And, 'Whoever swears by the altar, it is nothing; but whoever swears by the gift that is on it, he is obliged to perform it.' Fools and blind! For which is greater, the gift or the altar that sanctifies the gift? Therefore he who swears by the altar, swears by it and by all things on it. He who swears by the temple, swears by it and by Him who dwells in it. And he who swears by heaven, swears by the throne of God and by Him who sits on it.

"Woe to you, scribes and Pharisees, hypocrites! For you pay tithe of mint and anise and cummin, and have neglected the weightier matters of the law: justice and mercy and faith. These you ought to have done, without leaving the others undone. Blind guides, who strain out a gnat and swallow a camel!

"Woe to you, scribes and Pharisees, hypocrites! For you cleanse the outside of the cup and dish, but inside they are full of extortion and self-indulgence. Blind Pharisee, first cleanse the inside of the cup and dish, that the outside of them may be clean also.

"Woe to you, scribes and Pharisees, hypocrites! For you are like whitewashed tombs which indeed appear beautiful outwardly, but inside are full of dead men's bones and all uncleanness. Even so you also outwardly appear righteous to men, but inside you are full of hypocrisy and lawlessness.

"Woe to you, scribes and Pharisees, hypocrites! Because you build the tombs of the prophets and adorn the monuments of the righteous, and say, 'If we had lived in the days of our fathers, we would not have been partakers with them in the blood of the prophets.'

"Therefore you are witnesses against yourselves that you are sons of those who murdered the prophets. Fill up, then, the measure of your fathers' guilt. Serpents, brood of vipers! How can you escape the condemnation of hell? Therefore, indeed, I send you prophets, wise men, and scribes: some of them you will kill and crucify, and some of them you will scourge in your synagogues and persecute from city to city, that on you may come all the righteous blood shed on the earth, from the blood of righteous Abel to the blood of Zechariah, son of Berechiah, whom you murdered between the temple and the altar. Assuredly, I say to you, all these things will come upon this generation."

Jesus Laments over Jerusalem

O Jerusalem, Jerusalem, the one who kills the prophets and stones those who are sent to her! How often I wanted to gather your children together, as a hen gathers her chicks under her wings, but you were not willing!

See! Your house is left to you desolate; for I say to you, you shall see Me no more till you say, "Blessed is He who comes in the name of the LORD!"

John 8:44

You are of your father the devil, and the desires of *your* father you want to do. He was a murderer from the beginning, and does not stand in the truth, because there is no truth in him. When he speaks a lie, he speaks from his own *resources*, for he is a liar and the father of it.

Matthew 3:1–7

In those days John the Baptist came preaching in the wilderness of Judea, and saying, "Repent, for the kingdom of heaven is at hand!" For this is he who was spoken of by the prophet Isaiah, saying:

"The voice of one crying in the wilderness: 'Prepare the way of the LORD;

Make His paths straight.'"

Now John himself was clothed in camel's hair, with a leather belt around his waist; and his food was locusts and wild honey. Then Jerusalem, all Judea, and all the region around the Jordan went out to him and were baptized by him in the Jordan, confessing their sins.

But when he saw many of the Pharisees and Sadducees coming to his baptism, he said to them, "Brood of vipers! Who warned you to flee from the wrath to come?"

Mark 1:4

John came baptizing in the wilderness and preaching a baptism of repentance for the remission of sins.

Luke 3:3

And he went into all the region around the Jordan, preaching a baptism of repentance for the remission of sins.

Matthew 3:7

But when he saw many of the Pharisees and Sadducees coming to his baptism, he said to them, "Brood of vipers! Who warned you to flee from the wrath to come?"

Luke 7:30

But the Pharisees and lawyers rejected the will of God for themselves, not having been baptized by him.

Matthew 23:35–36

That on you may come all the righteous blood shed on the earth, from the blood of righteous Abel to the blood of Zechariah, son of Berechiah, whom you murdered between the temple and the altar. 36 Assuredly, I say to you, all these things will come upon this generation.

Exodus 29:4

And Aaron and his sons you shall bring to the door of the tabernacle of meeting, and you shall wash them with water.

Exodus 19:5–6

"Now therefore, if you will indeed obey My voice and keep My covenant, then you shall be a special treasure to Me above all people; for all the earth *is* Mine. And you shall be to Me a kingdom of priests and a holy nation." These *are* the words which you shall speak to the children of Israel.

Isaiah 61:6–9

But you shall be named the priests of the LORD,

They shall call you the servants of our God.

You shall eat the riches of the Gentiles, And in their glory you shall boast.

Instead of your shame you shall have double honor, And instead of confusion they shall rejoice in their portion. Therefore in their land they shall possess double; Everlasting joy shall be theirs.

"For I, the LORD, love justice; I hate robbery for burnt offering; I will direct their work in truth, And will make with them an everlasting covenant.

Their descendants shall be known among the Gentiles, And their offspring among the people.

All who see them shall acknowledge them, That they are the posterity whom the LORD has blessed."

NOTES

THE MINISTRY OF CHRIST TO ISRAEL

Jesus Christ was the *Son* of God, the Messiah, the king promised to Israel in the Old Testament. He preached *to Israel* "the gospel of the kingdom," which was, "The time is fulfilled, and **the kingdom of God is at hand.**"[85]

Christ was "a minister **of the circumcision**...to confirm the promises *made* unto the fathers,"[86] and He said, "I am not sent but **unto the lost sheep of the house of Israel.**"[87]

Christ taught that salvation was through Him. Those who believed that He was "the Son of God...the King of Israel" would receive eternal life, to be realized in the kingdom.[88] And He also taught obedience to the Law of Moses that had been given to Israel.[89]

Christ went to Israel because, according to prophecy, Israel was to be the channel of blessing to the Gentiles. Christ came to Israel, not to exclude the Gentiles, but in order to reach the Gentiles through Israel's rise to kingdom glory.

At the time of Christ's earthly ministry, the Abrahamic covenant was still in effect. To be blessed, Gentiles had to bless Israel and believe the kingdom gospel. Study the two Gentiles who are blessed in the gospels.

---

[85] Mark 1:14–15, Matthew 4:17.
[86] Romans 15:8.
[87] Matthew 15:24.
[88] John 1:49 and 20:31; Matthew 16:16; Luke 12:32.
[89] Matthew 5:19, 8:4, 23:1–3; Luke 5:14.

The centurion in Luke 7:2–5 was blessed because he sent elders of the *Jews* to Jesus to ask for the healing of his servant. The Jews told Christ that He was worthy, "**For he loveth our nation, and he hath built us a synagogue**."

The woman of Canaan in Matthew 15:22–28 did not receive healing until she acknowledged that she understood her place as a Gentile under the Abrahamic covenant. When Christ said to her, "It is not meet to take the children's [Israel's] bread, and to cast *it* to dogs [Gentiles]," she responded, "Truth, Lord: yet the dogs eat of the crumbs which fall from their masters' table."

Scripture Verses

Mark 1:14–15

Now after John was put in prison, Jesus came to Galilee, preaching the gospel of the kingdom of God, and saying, "The time is fulfilled, and the kingdom of God is at hand. Repent, and believe in the gospel."

Matthew 4:17

From that time Jesus began to preach and to say, "Repent, for the kingdom of heaven is at hand."

Romans 15:8

Now I say that Jesus Christ has become a servant to the circumcision for the truth of God, to confirm the promises made to the fathers.

Matthew 15:24

But He answered and said, "I was not sent except to the lost sheep of the house of Israel."

John 1:49

Nathanael answered and said to Him, "Rabbi, You are the Son of God! You are the King of Israel!"

John 20:31

But these are written that you may believe that Jesus is the Christ, the Son of God, and that believing you may have life in His name.

Matthew 16:16

Simon Peter answered and said, "You are the Christ, the Son of the living God.

Luke 12:32

Do not fear, little flock, for it is your Father's good pleasure to give you the kingdom.

Matthew 5:19

Whoever therefore breaks one of the least of these commandments, and teaches men so, shall be called least in the kingdom of heaven; but who-

ever does and teaches *them*, he shall be called great in the kingdom of heaven. For I say to you, that unless your righteousness exceeds *the righteousness* of the scribes and Pharisees, you will by no means enter the kingdom of heaven.

Matthew 8:4

And Jesus said to him, "See that you tell no one; but go your way, show yourself to the priest, and offer the gift that Moses commanded, as a testimony to them."

Matthew 23:1–3

Then Jesus spoke to the multitudes and to His disciples, saying: "The scribes and the Pharisees sit in Moses' seat. Therefore whatever they tell you to observe, *that* observe and do, but do not do according to their works; for they say, and do not do."

Luke 5:14

And He charged him to tell no one, "But go and show yourself to the priest, and make an offering for your cleansing, as a testimony to them, just as Moses commanded."

NOTES

THE SIGNS OF THE KINGDOM

During His earthly ministry, Jesus Christ worked miracles to validate that He was the Messiah, God in the flesh. His miracles gave the people a foretaste of the coming kingdom.

The two hallmark signs of the kingdom were casting out devils and healing the sick. These signs fill the gospels. Christ said, "If I with the finger of God cast out devils, no doubt the kingdom of God is come upon you."[90] In casting out devils, He was demonstrating His capacity to bind the strong man (Satan) and spoil His house (the house of Israel).[91] He was demonstrating that He was the one who would rescue Israel from Satanic captivity.[92]

When asked, "Art thou He that should come?" Christ answered by quoting a passage about the kingdom, "The blind receive their sight, and the lame walk, the lepers are cleansed, and the deaf hear, the dead are raised up."[93]

His miracles were a demonstration that He was God in their midst and the kingdom was indeed at hand.

---

90   Luke 11:20.
91   Matthew 12:29.
92   Isaiah 49:24–25.
93   Matthew 11:3–6 with Isaiah 35:5–6.

Scripture Verses

Luke 11:20

But if I cast out demons with the finger of God, surely the kingdom of God has come upon you.

Matthew 12:29

Or how can one enter a strong man's house and plunder his goods, unless he first binds the strong man? And then he will plunder his house.

Isaiah 49:24–25

Shall the prey be taken from the mighty, or the lawful captive delivered?

But thus saith the LORD: "Even the captives of the mighty shall be taken away, and the prey of the terrible shall be delivered; for I will contend with him that contendeth with thee, and I will save thy children."

Matthew 11:3–6

And said to Him, "Are You the Coming One, or do we look for another?"

Jesus answered and said to them, "Go and tell John the things which you hear and see: *The* blind see and the lame walk; *the* lepers are cleansed and *the* deaf hear; *the* dead are raised up and *the* poor have the gospel preached to them. And blessed is he who is not offended because of Me."

Isaiah 35:5–6

Then the eyes of the blind shall be opened,

And the ears of the deaf shall be unstopped.

Then the lame shall leap like a deer, And the tongue of the dumb sing.

For waters shall burst forth in the wilderness,

And streams in the desert.

NOTES

CHRIST TEACHES ABOUT THE KINGDOM

C hrist's earthly ministry focused on the kingdom promised to Israel in the Old Testament. In what is called the "Sermon on the Mount," Christ taught about the nature of this kingdom and those who will enter it.

He exalted the law because, once the kingdom is established, the law will be magnified and enforced on earth.[94] The law will be written on redeemed Israel's hearts, and God says He will "cause you [Israel] to walk in my statutes."[95]

Jesus Christ also said the meek "shall inherit **the earth**."[96] He taught Israel to pray, "**Thy kingdom come.** Thy will be done **in earth**."[97]

In the parables, He taught about different aspects of the kingdom. For example, in the parable in Luke 19:12–27, He taught that a nobleman (Jesus Christ) went "to a far country" (heaven) to "receive for himself a kingdom, and to return." (Note Daniel 7:13–14 and Revelation 21:2, 10.) Upon His return, those who were faithful were given cities in the kingdom to rule over, as the faithful in Israel will be given in the kingdom.[98]

In the parable of the householder and his vineyard, Matthew 21:33–45, Christ reveals that the kingdom will be taken from the apostate religious leaders of Israel and given to a nation (singular—

---

94 Matthew 5:17–48 with Isaiah 42:21.
95 Jeremiah 31:33; Ezekiel 36:27; Isaiah 2:3.
96 Matthew 5:5; Psalm 37:9–11.
97 Matthew 6:10.
98 Obadiah 19–21; Psalms 69:35–36; Isaiah 54:3, 61:4–5.

the believing remnant in Israel, "the little flock"[99]) bringing forth the fruits thereof. Note how Isaiah 5:1–7 explains this parable. Israel is the vineyard of God.

---

[99] Luke 12:32.

Scripture Verses

Matthew 5:17–48

Do not think that I came to destroy the Law or the Prophets. I did not come to destroy but to fulfill. For assuredly, I say to you, till heaven and earth pass away, one jot or one tittle will by no means pass from the law till all is fulfilled. Whoever therefore breaks one of the least of these commandments, and teaches men so, shall be called least in the kingdom of heaven; but whoever does and teaches *them*, he shall be called great in the kingdom of heaven. For I say to you, that unless your righteousness exceeds *the righteousness* of the scribes and Pharisees, you will by no means enter the kingdom of heaven.

Murder Begins in the Heart

"You have heard that it was said to those of old, 'You shall not murder, and whoever murders will be in danger of the judgment.'

But I say to you that whoever is angry with his brother without a cause shall be in danger of the judgment. And whoever says to his brother, 'Raca!' shall be in danger of the council. But whoever says, 'You fool!' shall be in danger of hell fire. Therefore if you bring your gift to the altar, and there remember that your brother has something against you, leave your gift there before the altar, and go your way. First be reconciled to your brother, and then come and offer your gift. Agree with your adversary quickly, while you are on the way with him, lest your adversary deliver you to the judge, the judge hand you over to the officer, and you be thrown into prison.

Assuredly, I say to you, you will by no means get out of there till you have paid the last penny.

Adultery in the Heart

"You have heard that it was said to those of old, 'You shall not commit adultery.' But I say to you that whoever looks at a woman to lust for her has already committed adultery with her in his heart. If your right eye causes you to sin, pluck it out and cast *it* from you; for it is more profitable for you that one of your members perish, than for your whole body to be cast into hell. And if your right hand causes you to sin, cut it off and cast *it* from you; for it is more profitable for you that one of your members perish, than for your whole body to be cast into hell.

Marriage Is Sacred and Binding

"Furthermore it has been said, 'Whoever divorces his wife, let him give her a certificate of divorce.' But I say to you that whoever divorces his wife for any reason except sexual immorality causes her to commit adultery; and whoever marries a woman who is divorced commits adultery.

Jesus Forbids Oaths

"Again you have heard that it was said to those of old, 'You shall not swear falsely, but shall perform your oaths to the Lord.'

But I say to you, do not swear at all: neither by heaven, for it is God's throne; nor by the earth, for it is His footstool; nor by Jerusalem, for it is the city of the great King. Nor shall you swear by your head, because you cannot make one hair white or black. But let your 'Yes' be 'Yes,' and your 'No,' 'No.' For whatever is more than these is from the evil one.

Go the Second Mile

"You have heard that it was said, 'An eye for an eye and a tooth for a tooth.' But I tell you not to resist an evil person. But whoever slaps you on your right cheek, turn the other to him also. If anyone wants to sue you and take away your tunic, let him have *your* cloak also.

And whoever compels you to go one mile, go with him two. Give to him who asks you, and from him who wants to borrow from you do not turn away.

Love Your Enemies

"You have heard that it was said, 'You shall love your neighbor and hate your enemy.' But

I say to you, love your enemies, bless those who curse you, do good to those who hate you, and pray for those who spitefully use you and persecute you, that you may be sons of your Father in heaven; for He makes His sun rise on the evil and on the good, and sends rain on the just and on the unjust. For if you love those who love you, what reward have you? Do not even the tax collectors do the same?

And if you greet your brethren only, what do you do more than others? Do not even the tax collectors do so? Therefore you shall be perfect, just as your Father in heaven is perfect.

Isaiah 42:21

The LORD is well pleased for His righteousness' sake;

He will exalt the law and make *it* honorable.

Jeremiah 31:33

But this is the covenant that I will make with the house of Israel after those days, says the LORD: I will put My law in their minds, and write it on their hearts; and I will be their God, and they shall be My people.

Ezekiel 36:27

I will put My Spirit within you and cause you to walk in My statutes, and you will keep My judgments and do *them*.

Isaiah 2:3

Many people shall come and say, "Come, and let us go up to the mountain of the LORD,

To the house of the God of Jacob; He will teach us His ways,

And we shall walk in His paths."

For out of Zion shall go forth the law, And the word of the LORD from Jerusalem.

Matthew 5:5

Blessed are the meek, For they shall inherit the earth.

Psalm 37:9–11

For evildoers shall be cut off; But those who wait on the LORD, They shall inherit the earth.

For yet a little while and the wicked *shall be* no *more*;

Indeed, you will look carefully for his place,

But it *shall be* no *more*.

But the meek shall inherit the earth,

And shall delight themselves in the abundance of peace.

Matthew 6:10

Your kingdom come. Your will be done.

Obadiah 19–21

The South shall possess the mountains of Esau,

And the Lowland shall possess Philistia. They shall possess the fields of Ephraim and the fields of Samaria.

Benjamin *shall possess* Gilead. And the captives of this host of the children of Israel *shall possess* the land of the Canaanites As far as Zarephath.

The captives of Jerusalem who are in Sepharad shall possess the cities of the South.

Then saviors shall come to Mount Zion To judge the mountains of Esau,

And the kingdom shall be the LORD's.

Psalm 69:35–36

For God will save Zion

And build the cities of Judah,

That they may dwell there and possess it.

Also, the descendants of His servants shall inherit it,

And those who love His name shall dwell in it.

Isaiah 54:3

For you shall expand to the right and to the left,

And your descendants will inherit the nations,

And make the desolate cities inhabited.

Isaiah 61:4–5

And they shall rebuild the old ruins,

They shall raise up the former desolations, And they shall repair the ruined cities, The desolations of many generations.

Strangers shall stand and feed your flocks,

And the sons of the foreigner

Luke 12:32

Do not fear, little flock, for it is your Father's good pleasure to give you the kingdom.

NOTES

CHRIST PREPARES ISRAEL
FOR THE TRIBULATION THAT
WILL PRECEDE THE KINGDOM

D uring His earthly ministry, Jesus Christ prepared His disciples for the coming of the tribulation period that will purge Israel prior to the kingdom.

For example, He told them that when they see the abomination of desolation spoken of by Daniel, they must flee to the mountains.[100] He told them to take no thought for what they shall eat or drink because God would take care of them.[101] He told them to sell that they had[102] (which believers did in Acts 2–4). All these instructions were given because, during the tribulation, they will have to flee from the Antichrist.[103] In the mountains, God will provide miraculously for them[104] just as He did for their fathers in the wilderness with *daily manna* and quail, and for Elijah when he fled from King Ahab.[105] That's why Christ told them to pray, "Give us this day our **daily bread.**"[106]

Christ further taught that after the tribulation, He would come with His angels to gather His elect (believers of Israel) into their land.[107] Matthew 13:41–42 says,

---

[100] Matthew 24:15–16.
[101] Matthew 6:31.
[102] Matthew 6:31.
[103] Matthew 24:16.
[104] Revelation 12:13–17.
[105] Exodus 16:15 and 1 Kings 17:4–6.
[106] Matthew 6:11.
[107] Matthew 24:27–31.

The Son of man shall send forth His angels, and they shall gather out of His kingdom all things that offend, and them which do iniquity; And shall cast them into a furnace of fire... Then shall the righteous shine forth as the sun in the kingdom of their Father.[108]

---

[108] See also Psalm 37:9 and Luke 17:34–37.

Scripture Verses

Matthew 24:15–16

When ye therefore shall see the abomination of desolation, spoken of by Daniel the prophet, stand in the holy place, (whoso readeth, let him understand:)

Then let them which be in Judaea flee into the mountains:

Matthew 6:31

Therefore take no thought, saying, What shall we eat? or, What shall we drink? or, Wherewithal shall we be clothed?

Luke 12:33

Sell that ye have, and give alms; provide yourselves bags which wax not old, a treasure in the heavens that faileth not, where no thief approacheth, neither moth corrupteth.

Matthew 24:16

Then let them which be in Judaea flee into the mountains:

Revelation 12:13–17

And when the dragon saw that he was cast unto the earth, he persecuted the woman which brought forth the man child.

And to the woman were given two wings of a great eagle, that she might fly into the wilderness, into her place, where she is nourished for a time, and times, and half a time, from the face of the serpent.

And the serpent cast out of his mouth water as a flood after the woman, that he might cause her to be carried away of the flood.

And the earth helped the woman, and the earth opened her mouth, and swallowed up the flood which the dragon cast out of his mouth.

And the dragon was wroth with the woman, and went to make war with the remnant of her seed, which keep the commandments of God, and have the testimony of Jesus Christ.

Exodus 16:15

And when the children of Israel saw it, they said one to another, It is manna: for they wist not what it was. And Moses said unto them, This is the bread which the LORD hath given you to eat.

1 Kings 17:4–6

And it shall be, that thou shalt drink of the brook; and I have commanded the ravens to feed thee there.

So he went and did according unto the word of the LORD: for he went and dwelt by the brook Cherith, that is before Jordan.

And the ravens brought him bread and flesh in the morning, and bread and flesh in the evening; and he drank of the brook.

Matthew 6:11

Give us this day our daily bread.

Matthew 24:27–31

For as the lightning cometh out of the east, and shineth even unto the west; so shall also the coming of the Son of man be.

For wheresoever the carcase is, there will the eagles be gathered together.

Immediately after the tribulation of those days shall the sun be darkened, and the moon shall not give her light, and the stars shall fall from heaven, and the powers of the heavens shall be shaken:

And then shall appear the sign of the Son of man in heaven: and then shall all the tribes of the earth mourn, and they shall see the Son of man coming in the clouds of heaven with power and great glory.

And he shall send his angels with a great sound of a trumpet, and they shall gather together his elect from the four winds, from one end of heaven to the other.

Psalm 37:9

For evildoers shall be cut off: but those that wait upon the LORD, they shall inherit the earth.

Luke 17:34–37

I tell you, in that night there shall be two men in one bed; the one shall be taken, and the other shall be left.

Two women shall be grinding together; the one shall be taken, and the other left.

Two men shall be in the field; the one shall be taken, and the other left.

And they answered and said unto him, Where, Lord? And he said unto them,

Wheresoever the body is, thither will the eagles be gathered together.

NOTES

CHRIST'S TWELVE APOSTLES PREACH "THE KINGDOM OF GOD IS AT HAND"

In preparation for the kingdom, Christ chose twelve apostles. He told them, "When the Son of man shall sit in the throne of His glory, ye also shall sit upon twelve thrones, judging the twelve tribes of Israel."[109] They were to be His cabinet, so to speak. He sent these twelve to preach *to Israel only*, "The kingdom of heaven is at hand."[110] He gave them power to work miracles, the signs of the kingdom.[111]

Note that "the gospel of the kingdom" preached by Christ and His apostles is *not* the gospel we preach today. For one thing, those who believed the gospel were promised eternal life in the kingdom God will establish on this earth, not eternal life in heaven.

In addition, when the apostles preached "the gospel of the kingdom," *they did not preach the cross*, which is central to the gospel today. They did not yet understand that Christ would have to die and be raised. In fact, late in their ministry, when Christ began to tell them of His coming death, Peter responded by saying, "Be it far from thee, Lord: this shall **not** be unto thee."[112] Additionally the scriptures are careful to tell us that "they **understood none** of these things: and this saying was **hid from them**, neither knew they the things which were spoken."[113] *Please carefully compare Luke 9:1–6 with Luke 18:32–34, Matthew 16:21–22 and 17:22–23, and Mark 9:9–10.*

109   Matthew 19:28; Isaiah 1:26.
110   Matthew 10:5–7.
111   Matthew 10:8; Hebrews 2:3–4.
112   Matthew 16:22.
113   Luke 18:34.

Scripture Verses

Matthew 19:28

And Jesus said unto them, Verily I say unto you, That ye which have followed me, in the regeneration when the Son of man shall sit in the throne of his glory, ye also shall sit upon twelve thrones, judging the twelve tribes of Israel.

Isaiah 1:26

And I will restore thy judges as at the first, and thy counsellors as at the beginning: afterward thou shalt be called, The city of righteousness, the faithful city.

Matthew 10:5–7

These twelve Jesus sent forth, and commanded them, saying, Go not into the way of the Gentiles, and into any city of the Samaritans enter ye not:

But go rather to the lost sheep of the house of Israel.

And as ye go, preach, saying, The kingdom of heaven is at hand.

Matthew 10:8

Heal the sick, cleanse the lepers, raise the dead, cast out devils: freely ye have received, freely give.

Hebrews 2:3–4

How shall we escape, if we neglect so great salvation; which at the first began to be spoken by the Lord, and was confirmed unto us by them that heard him;

God also bearing them witness, both with signs and wonders, and with divers miracles, and gifts of the Holy Ghost, according to his own will?

Matthew 16:22

Then Peter took him, and began to rebuke him, saying, Be it far from thee, Lord: this shall not be unto thee.

Luke 18:34

And they understood none of these things: and this saying was hid from them, neither knew they the things which were spoken.

NOTES

ISRAEL REJECTS HER KING

The leaders of Israel, under Satan's influence,[114] rejected Christ and called for His crucifixion. Jesus Christ went willingly, trusting the will of the Father.[115] (The fulfillment of Israel's Feast of Passover. See page 63.) God raised Him from the dead after three days. (Fulfillment of the Feast of Firstfruits, p. 28.)

The risen Christ then appeared to the apostles and gave them the Holy Ghost so that they would have the authority and understanding to carry on His ministry after His ascension.[116] Luke 24:45 says that Christ "opened their understanding." Acts 1:3 says that He spent forty days with them, "speaking of the things **pertaining to the kingdom of God.**" So in Acts 1:6, the apostles asked, "Lord, wilt thou at this time restore again the **kingdom to Israel?**"

He told them that it was not for them to know the times, but that they "shall be witnesses unto me both in Jerusalem, and in all Judaea, and in Samaria [the land promised to Israel], and unto the uttermost part of the earth."[117] But Christ had told them that they will not have gone over all the cities of Israel before He would return.[118] This is because, under the prophesied plan, Israel as a nation had to be cleansed during the tribulation, then Christ would come and send redeemed Israel to the Gentiles. So the apostles remained in Jerusalem throughout the early Acts period, preaching *to the Jews* and proselytes, calling on them to repent.[119]

[114] John 8:44.
[115] Acts 2:23; Matthew 26:39; Isaiah 50:5–9.
[116] John 20:21–23, 14:26, 16:13.
[117] Acts 1:8.
[118] Matthew 10:23.
[119] Acts 2:10, 14, 22–40; 5:30–31; 8:1.

Scripture Verses

John 8:44

Ye are of your father the devil, and the lusts of your father ye will do. He was a murderer from the beginning, and abode not in the truth, because there is no truth in him. When he speaketh a lie, he speaketh of his own: for he is a liar, and the father of it.

Acts 2:23

Him, being delivered by the determinate counsel and foreknowledge of God, ye have taken, and by wicked hands have crucified and slain.

Matthew 26:39

And he went a little farther, and fell on his face, and prayed, saying, O my Father, if it be possible, let this cup pass from me: nevertheless not as I will, but as thou wilt.

Isaiah 50:5–9

The Lord GOD hath opened mine ear, and I was not rebellious, neither turned away back.

I gave my back to the smiters, and my cheeks to them that plucked off the hair: I hid not my face from shame and spitting.

For the Lord GOD will help me; therefore shall I not be confounded: therefore have I set my face like a flint, and I know that I shall not be ashamed.

He is near that justifieth me; who will contend with me? let us stand together: who is mine adversary? let him come near to me.

Behold, the Lord GOD will help me; who is he that shall condemn me? lo, they all shall wax old as a garment; the moth shall eat them up.

John 20:21-23

Then said Jesus to them again, Peace be unto you: as my Father hath sent me, even so send I you. And when he had said this, he breathed on them, and saith unto them, Receive ye the Holy Ghost:

Whose soever sins ye remit, they are remitted unto them; and whose soever sins ye retain, they are retained.

John 14:26

But the Comforter, which is the Holy Ghost, whom the Father will send in my name, he shall teach you all things, and bring all things to your remembrance, whatsoever I have said unto you.

John 16:13

Howbeit when he, the Spirit of truth, is come, he will guide you into all truth: for he shall not speak of himself; but whatsoever he shall hear, that shall he speak: and he will shew you things to come.

Acts 1:8

But ye shall receive power, after that the Holy Ghost is come upon you: and ye shall be witnesses unto me both in Jerusalem, and in all Judaea, and in Samaria, and unto the uttermost part of the earth.

Matthew 10:23

But when they persecute you in this city, flee ye into another: for verily I say unto you, Ye shall not have gone over the cities of Israel, till the Son of man be come.

Acts 2:10, 14, 22–40

Phrygia, and Pamphylia, in Egypt, and in the parts of Libya about Cyrene, and strangers of Rome, Jews and proselytes,

But Peter, standing up with the eleven, lifted up his voice, and said unto them, Ye men of Judaea, and all ye that dwell at Jerusalem, be this known unto you, and hearken to my words:

Ye men of Israel, hear these words; Jesus of Nazareth, a man approved of God among you by miracles and wonders and signs, which God did by him in the midst of you, as ye yourselves also know:

Him, being delivered by the determinate counsel and foreknowledge of God, ye have taken, and by wicked hands have crucified and slain:

Whom God hath raised up, having loosed the pains of death: because it was not possible that he should be holden of it.

For David speaketh concerning him, I foresaw the Lord always before my face, for he is on my right hand, that I should not be moved:

Therefore did my heart rejoice, and my tongue was glad; moreover also my flesh shall rest in hope:

Because thou wilt not leave my soul in hell, neither wilt thou suffer thine Holy One to see corruption.

Thou hast made known to me the ways of life; thou shalt make me full of joy with thy countenance.

Men and brethren, let me freely speak unto you

Of the patriarch David, that he is both dead and buried, and his sepulchre is with us unto this day.

Therefore being a prophet, and knowing that God had sworn with an oath to him, that of the fruit of

His loins, according to the flesh, he would raise up. Christ to sit on his throne;

He seeing this before spake of the resurrection of Christ, that his soul was not left in hell, neither his flesh did see corruption.

This Jesus hath God raised up, whereof we all are witnesses.

Therefore being by the right hand of God exalted, and having received of the Father the promise of the Holy Ghost, he hath shed forth this, which ye now see and hear.

For David is not ascended into the heavens: but he saith himself, The Lord said unto my Lord, Sit thou on my right hand,

Until I make thy foes thy footstool.

Therefore let all the house of Israel know assuredly, that God hath made the same Jesus, whom ye have crucified, both Lord and Christ.

Now when they heard this, they were pricked in their heart, and said unto Peter and to the rest of the apostles, Men and brethren, what shall we do?

Then Peter said unto them, Repent, and be baptized every one of you in the name of Jesus Christ for the remission of sins, and ye shall receive the gift of the Holy Ghost.

For the promise is unto you, and to your children, and to all that are afar off, even as many as the LORD our God shall call.

And with many other words did he testify and exhort, saying, Save yourselves from this untoward generation.

Acts 5:30–31

The God of our fathers raised up Jesus, whom ye slew and hanged on a tree.

Him hath God exalted with his right hand to be a Prince and a Saviour, for to give repentance to Israel, and forgiveness of sins.

Acts 8:1

And Saul was consenting unto his death. And at that time there was a great persecution against the church which was at Jerusalem; and they were all scattered abroad throughout the regions of Judaea and Samaria, except the apostles.

NOTES

Israel's Last Chance
The Witness of the
Holy Ghost

F rom the cross, Christ had prayed, "Father, forgive them; for
they know not what they do."[120] After His ascension, He sent
the Holy Ghost to fill the apostles and disciples with power
from on high.[121] (This was also the fulfillment of the Jewish Feast
of Pentecost—it had "fully come.") In Acts 2–5, the Holy Ghost,
through Peter, gave the men of Israel one last chance to repent of
rejecting their Christ.

Peter says that Pentecost (Acts 2) was *"the last days"* prior to the
kingdom, as prophesied by Joel.[122] (It is *not* said to be the *first* days
of the body of Christ.) Pentecost was one of the three times each year
when Jewish men from every nation came to Jerusalem. These Jews
were Peter's audience. (Acts 2:10.) The Holy Ghost, through Peter,
indicted them for the rejection and crucifixion of their own Messiah.
He said that they "by wicked hands have crucified and slain" the
"Prince of life."[123] Peter tells the men of Israel, "Repent, and **be baptized** every one of you in the name of Jesus Christ **for the remission
of sins**...Save yourselves from this untoward generation."[124] (Note
that the "generation" he is referring to is the "generation of vipers,"
the apostate leaders of Israel—Matthew 23:33–37.)

---

[120] Luke 23:34.
[121] Luke 24:49; Acts 2:4.
[122] Acts 2:16–17; Joel 2:28–32.
[123] Acts 2:22–24, 3:15, 5:30.
[124] Acts 2:38–40.

Peter says, "Repent… And He shall send Jesus Christ, which before was preached unto you: Whom the heaven must receive until the times of restitution of all things [the kingdom], which God hath spoken by the mouth of all His holy prophets since the world began."[125] He reminds them, "**Ye** are the children of the prophets, and of the covenant which God made with our fathers."[126]

The apostles worked miracles to validate their message and enlighten Israel.[127] But most of the leaders refused to believe and persecuted the apostles.

---

[125] Acts 3:19–21.
[126] Acts 3:25.
[127] Acts 3:1–11; Hebrews 2:3–4.

Scripture Verses

Luke 23:34

And Pilate gave sentence that it should be as they required.

Luke 24:49

And, behold, I send the promise of my Father upon you: but tarry ye in the city of Jerusalem, until ye be endued with power from on high.

Acts 2:4

And they were all filled with the Holy Ghost, and began to speak with other tongues, as the Spirit gave them utterance.

Acts 2:16–17

But this is that which was spoken by the prophet Joel;

And it shall come to pass in the last days, saith God, I will pour out of my Spirit upon all flesh: and your sons and your daughters shall prophesy, and your young men shall see visions, and your old men shall dream dreams.

Joel 2:28–32

And it shall come to pass afterward, that I will pour out my spirit upon all flesh; and your sons and your daughters shall prophesy, your old men shall dream dreams, your young men shall see visions:

And also upon the servants and upon the handmaids in those days will I pour out my spirit.

And I will shew wonders in the heavens and in the earth, blood, and fire, and pillars of smoke.

The sun shall be turned into darkness, and the moon into blood, before the great and terrible day of the LORD come.

And it shall come to pass, that whosoever shall call on the name of the LORD shall be delivered: for in mount Zion and in Jerusalem shall be deliverance, as the LORD hath said, and in the remnant whom the LORD shall call.

Acts 2:22–24

Ye men of Israel, hear these words; Jesus of Nazareth, a man approved of God among you by miracles and wonders and signs, which God did by him in the midst of you, as ye yourselves also know:

Him, being delivered by the determinate counsel and foreknowledge of God, ye have taken, and by wicked hands have crucified and slain:

Whom God hath raised up, having loosed the pains of death: because it was not possible that he should be holden of it.

Acts 3:15

And killed the Prince of life, whom God hath raised from the dead; whereof we are witnesses.

Acts 5:30

The God of our fathers raised up Jesus, whom ye slew and hanged on a tree.

Acts 2:38–40

Then Peter said unto them, Repent, and be baptized every one of you in the name of Jesus Christ for the remission of sins, and ye shall receive the gift of the Holy Ghost.

For the promise is unto you, and to your children, and to all that are afar off, even as many as the LORD our God shall call.

And with many other words did he testify and exhort, saying, Save yourselves from this untoward generation.

Acts 3:19-21

Repent ye therefore, and be converted, that your sins may be blotted out, when the times of refreshing shall come from the presence of the Lord.

And he shall send Jesus Christ, which before was preached unto you:

Whom the heaven must receive until the times of restitution of all things, which God hath spoken by the mouth of all his holy prophets since the world began.

Acts 3:25

Ye are the children of the prophets, and of the covenant which God made with our fathers, saying unto Abraham, And in thy seed shall all the kindreds of the earth be blessed.

Acts 3:1–11

Now Peter and John went up together into the temple at the hour of prayer, being the ninth hour.

And a certain man lame from his mother's womb was carried, whom they laid daily at the gate of the temple which is called Beautiful, to ask alms of them that entered into the temple;

Who seeing Peter and John about to go into the temple asked an alms.

And Peter, fastening his eyes upon him with John, said, Look on us.

And he gave heed unto them, expecting to receive something of them.

Then Peter said, Silver and gold have I none; but such as I have give I thee: In the name of Jesus Christ of Nazareth rise up and walk.

And he took him by the right hand, and lifted him up: and immediately his feet and ankle bones received strength.

And he leaping up stood, and walked, and entered with them into the temple, walking, and leaping, and praising God.

And all the people saw him walking and praising God:

And they knew that it was he which sat for alms at the Beautiful gate of the temple: and they were filled with wonder and amazement at that which had happened unto him.

And as the lame man which was healed held Peter and John, all the people ran together unto them in the porch that is called Solomon's, greatly wondering.

Hebrews 2:3–4

How shall we escape, if we neglect so great salvation; which at the first began to be spoken by the Lord, and was confirmed unto us by them that heard him;

God also bearing them witness, both with signs and wonders, and with divers miracles, and gifts of the Holy Ghost, according to his own will?

NOTES

THE FALL OF ISRAEL
THE BLASPHEMY OF
THE HOLY GHOST

B y this point, the leaders of Israel had *rejected God the Father* by rejecting the ministry of John the Baptist, "a man sent from God."[128]

They had *rejected God the Son* by calling for His crucifixion.

Now they were rejecting *God the Holy Ghost* by persecuting the apostles and disciples who were filled with and speaking by the Holy Ghost.[129] This "blasphemy of the Holy Ghost" Jesus Christ had said would not be forgiven.[130]

Their "blasphemy of the Holy Ghost" culminated with the stoning of Stephen.

As he was dying, he looked up into heaven and saw Jesus *standing*.[131] Prophecy says that the ascended Christ was to *sit* at the Father's right hand *until He made His enemies His footstool*.[132] The fact that Stephen saw Him *standing* indicated that Jesus Christ was ready to initiate the time of judgment.[133] And, indeed, the next prophesied event was the Great Tribulation, "the time of Jacob's trouble."[134]

Israel had fallen, and God's wrath was ready to be poured out.

---

[128] John 1:6.
[129] Acts 7:55–60.
[130] Matthew 12:31–32.
[131] Acts 7:55.
[132] Psalm 110:1 and Acts 2:34–35.
[133] Isaiah 2:19–21 and 3:13; Psalm 7:6, 9:19, 68:1, 82:8.
[134] Jeremiah 30:7.

Scripture Verses

John 1:6

There was a man sent from God, whose name was John.

Acts 7:55–60

But he, being full of the Holy Ghost, looked up stedfastly into heaven, and saw the glory of God, and Jesus standing on the right hand of God,

And said, Behold, I see the heavens opened, and the Son of man standing on the right hand of God.

Then they cried out with a loud voice, and stopped their ears, and ran upon him with one accord,

And cast him out of the city, and stoned him: and the witnesses laid down their clothes at a young man's feet, whose name was Saul.

And they stoned Stephen, calling upon God, and saying, Lord Jesus, receive my spirit.

And he kneeled down, and cried with a loud voice, Lord, lay not this sin to their charge. And when he had said this, he fell asleep.

Matthew 12:31–32

Wherefore I say unto you, All manner of sin and blasphemy shall be forgiven unto men: but the blasphemy against the Holy Ghost shall not be forgiven unto men.

And whosoever speaketh a word against the Son of man, it shall be forgiven him: but whosoever speaketh against the Holy Ghost, it shall not be forgiven him, neither in this world, neither in the world to come.

Acts 7:55

But he, being full of the Holy Ghost, looked up stedfastly into heaven, and saw the glory of God, and Jesus standing on the right hand of God.

Psalm 110:1

The LORD said unto my Lord, Sit thou at my right hand, until I make thine enemies thy footstool.

Acts 2:34–35

For David is not ascended into the heavens: but he saith himself, The Lord said unto my Lord, Sit thou on my right hand,

Until I make thy foes thy footstool.

Isaiah 2:19–21

And they shall go into the holes of the rocks, and into the caves of the earth, for fear of the LORD, and for the glory of his majesty, when he ariseth to shake terribly the earth.

In that day a man shall cast his idols of silver, and his idols of gold, which they made each one for himself to worship, to the moles and to the bats;

To go into the clefts of the rocks, and into the tops of the ragged rocks, for fear of the LORD, and for the glory of his majesty, when he ariseth to shake terribly the earth.

The LORD standeth up to plead, and standeth to judge the people.

Psalm 7:6

The LORD shall judge the people: judge me, O LORD, according to my righteousness, and according to mine integrity that is in me.

Psalm 9:19

Arise, O LORD; let not man prevail: let the heathen be judged in thy sight.

Psalm 68:1

Let God arise, let his enemies be scattered: let them also that hate him flee before him.

Psalm 82:8

Arise, O God, judge the earth: for thou shalt inherit all nations.

Jeremiah 30:7

Alas! for that day is great, so that none is like it: it is even the time of Jacob's trouble, but he shall be saved out of it.

NOTES

MID-ACTS AND PAUL'S EPISTLES (ROMANS–PHILEMON)

Prophecy Interrupted: God's Plan for the Heavens Revealed
(The Church, the Body of Christ, and the Mystery)

A NEW DISPENSATION
THE DISPENSATION OF
THE GRACE OF GOD

*B*ut God's wrath did not fall! The fulfillment of prophecy did not continue.

Why? What happened?

When Israel fell, rather than pour out His wrath, God interrupted the prophetic plan and poured out His grace. He did not let Israel's rejection of Christ stand in the way of Gentile salvation.[135] He reached down and saved the leader of the rebellion, Saul of Tarsus.[136] To Saul (the apostle Paul), He revealed the plan He had "kept secret since the world began"—"*the mystery.*"[137] In so doing, God began "the dispensation of grace"[138]—an offer of amnesty to the world.

Remember, when we discussed Lucifer's rebellion in heaven, we said that God had a plan to regain the heavens, but He kept it secret. With the salvation of Saul, God began to reveal it. God put His prophesied plan to restore the earth through Israel on hold temporarily[139] and began to initiate His secret plan to restore the heavenly places. We will see that, through Paul, He began to reveal that He would form a new agency—the Church, the Body of Christ—that will rule and reign with Him in heaven. This "new

---

[135] Romans 11:11.
[136] Acts 9:1–6, 22:1, 26:1–8; 1 Timothy 1:12–16.
[137] Ephesians 3:1–9 and Romans 16:25.
[138] Ephesians 3:2 and Colossians 1:25.
[139] Romans 11:15, 25–32.

creature" and its heavenly hope is the focus of what God calls "the mystery" that was hid in God, not revealed before it was made known through Paul.

Scripture Verses

Romans 11:11

I say then, Have they stumbled that they should fall? God forbid: but rather through their fall salvation is come unto the Gentiles, for to provoke them to jealousy.

Acts 9:1–6

And Saul, yet breathing out threatenings and slaughter against the disciples of the Lord, went unto the high priest,

And desired of him letters to Damascus to the synagogues, that if he found any of this way, whether they were men or women, he might bring them bound unto Jerusalem.

And as he journeyed, he came near Damascus: and suddenly there shined round about him a light from heaven:

And he fell to the earth, and heard a voice saying unto him, Saul, Saul, why persecutest thou me?

And he said, Who art thou, Lord? And the Lord said, I am Jesus whom thou persecutest: it is hard for thee to kick against the pricks.

And he trembling and astonished said, Lord, what wilt thou have me to do? And the Lord said unto him, Arise, and go into the city, and it shall be told thee what thou must do.

Acts 22:1–22

Men, brethren, and fathers, hear ye my defence which I make now unto you. (And when they heard that he spake in the Hebrew tongue to them, they kept the more silence: and he saith,)

I am verily a man which am a Jew, born in Tarsus, a city in Cilicia, yet brought up in this city at the feet of Gamaliel, and taught according to the perfect manner of the law of the fathers, and was zealous toward God, as ye all are this day.

And I persecuted this way unto the death, binding and delivering into prisons both men and women.

As also the high priest doth bear me witness, and all the estate of the elders: from whom also I received letters unto the brethren, and went to Damascus, to bring them which were there bound unto Jerusalem, for to be punished.

And it came to pass, that, as I made my journey, and was come nigh unto Damascus about noon, suddenly there shone from heaven a great light round about me.

And I fell unto the ground, and heard a voice saying unto me, Saul, Saul, why persecutest thou me?

And I answered, Who art thou, Lord? And he said unto me, I am Jesus of Nazareth, whom thou persecutest.

And they that were with me saw indeed the light, and were afraid; but they heard not the voice of him that spake to me.

And I said, What shall I do, LORD?

And the Lord said unto me, Arise, and go into Damascus; and there it shall be told thee of all things which are appointed for thee to do.

And when I could not see for the glory of that light, being led by the hand of them that were with me, I came into Damascus.

And one Ananias, a devout man according to the law, having a good report of all the Jews which dwelt there,

Came unto me, and stood, and said unto me, Brother Saul, receive thy sight. And the same hour I looked up upon him.

And he said, The God of our fathers hath chosen thee, that thou shouldest know his will, and see that Just One, and shouldest hear the voice of his mouth.

For thou shalt be his witness unto all men of what thou hast seen and heard.

And now why tarriest thou? arise, and be baptized, and wash away thy sins, calling on the name of the Lord.

And it came to pass, that, when I was come again to Jerusalem, even while I prayed in the temple, I was in a trance;

And saw him saying unto me, Make haste, and get thee quickly out of Jerusalem: for they will not receive thy testimony concerning me.

And I said, Lord, they know that I imprisoned and beat in every synagogue them that believed on thee:

And when the blood of thy martyr Stephen was shed, I also was standing by, and consenting unto his death, and kept the raiment of them that slew him.

And he said unto me, Depart: for I will send thee far hence unto the Gentiles.

And they gave him audience unto this word, and then lifted up their voices, and said, Away with such a fellow from the earth: for it is not fit that he should live.

Acts 26:1–8

Then Agrippa said unto Paul, Thou art permitted to speak for thyself. Then Paul stretched forth the hand, and answered for himself:

I think myself happy, king Agrippa, because I shall answer for myself this day before thee touching all the things whereof I am accused of the Jews:

Especially because I know thee to be expert in all customs and questions which are among the Jews: wherefore I beseech thee to hear me patiently.

My manner of life from my youth, which was at the first among mine own nation at Jerusalem, know all the Jews;

Which knew me from the beginning, if they would testify, that after the most straitest sect of our religion I lived a Pharisee.

And now I stand and am judged for the hope of the promise made of God, unto our fathers:

Unto which promise our twelve tribes, instantly serving God day and night, hope to come. For which hope's sake, king Agrippa, I am accused of the Jews.

Why should it be thought a thing incredible with you, that God should raise the dead?

1 Timothy 1:12–16

And I thank Christ Jesus our Lord, who hath enabled me, for that he counted me faithful, putting me into the ministry;

Who was before a blasphemer, and a persecutor, and injurious: but I obtained mercy, because I did it ignorantly in unbelief.

And the grace of our Lord was exceeding abundant with faith and love which is in Christ Jesus.

This is a faithful saying, and worthy of all acceptation, that Christ Jesus came into the world to save sinners; of whom I am chief.,

Howbeit for this cause I obtained mercy, that in me first Jesus Christ might shew forth all longsuffering, for a pattern to them which should hereafter believe on him to life everlasting.

Ephesians 3:1–9

For this cause I Paul, the prisoner of Jesus Christ for you Gentiles,

If ye have heard of the dispensation of the grace of God which is given me to you-ward:

How that by revelation he made known unto me the mystery; (as I wrote afore in few words,

Whereby, when ye read, ye may understand my knowledge in the mystery of Christ)

Which in other ages was not made known unto the sons of men, as it is now revealed unto his holy apostles and prophets by the Spirit;

That the Gentiles should be fellowheirs, and of the same body, and partakers of his promise in Christ by the gospel:

Whereof I was made a minister, according to the gift of the grace of God given unto me by the effectual working of his power.

Unto me, who am less than the least of all saints, is this grace given, that I should preach among the Gentiles the unsearchable riches of Christ;

And to make all men see what is the fellowship of the mystery, which from the beginning of the world hath been hid in God, who created all things by Jesus Christ.

Romans 16:25

Now to him that is of power to stablish you according to my gospel, and the preaching of Jesus Christ, according to the revelation of the mystery, which was kept secret since the world began.

Ephesians 3:2

For this cause I Paul, the prisoner of Jesus Christ for you Gentiles,

If ye have heard of the dispensation of the grace of God which is given me to you-ward: How that by revelation he made known unto me the mystery; (as I wrote afore in few words.

Colossians 1:25

Whereof I am made a minister, according to the dispensation of God which is given to me for you, to fulfil the word of God.

Romans 11:15, 25–32

For if the casting away of them be the reconciling of the world, what shall the receiving of them be, but life from the dead?

For I would not, brethren, that ye should be ignorant of this mystery, lest ye should be wise in your own conceits; that blindness in part is happened to Israel, until the fulness of the Gentiles be come in.

And so all Israel shall be saved: as it is written, There shall come out of Sion the Deliverer, and shall turn away ungodliness from Jacob:

For this is my covenant unto them, when I shall take away their sins.

As concerning the gospel, they are enemies for your sakes: but as touching the election, they are beloved for the father's sakes.

For the gifts and calling of God are without repentance.

For as ye in times past have not believed God, yet have now obtained mercy through their unbelief:

Even so have these also now not believed, that through your mercy they also may obtain mercy.

For God hath concluded them all in unbelief, that he might have mercy upon all.

THE REVELATION OF THE MYSTERY

The Old Testament spoke about, and the gospels focused on, God's plan to reclaim the earth through the kingdom promised to Israel. This plan had been *spoken about* "**by the mouth of His holy prophets, which have been since the world began.**"[140]

In early Acts, Peter tells Israel, "All the prophets from Samuel and those that follow after, as many as **have spoken**, have likewise foretold of these days."[141]

In contrast, the apostle Paul writes about God's plan to reclaim the *heavenly* places through the church, the body of Christ. He calls the things He speaks of the revelation of "the mystery." This is what he says in Ephesians 3:2–3:

> If ye have heard of the dispensation of the
> grace of God which is given me to you-ward:
> How that by revelation He made known unto
> me the mystery.[142]

Paul claims that the things he was sent to proclaim had been "**kept secret since the world began.**"[143] He said that His message "in other ages was **not made known** unto the sons of men"[144] but "from

---

[140] Luke 1:70.
[141] Acts 3:24.
[142] See also Colossians 1:25–26.
[143] Romans 16:25.
[144] Ephesians 3:5.

the beginning of the world hath been **hid in God**."[145] He said that God "**in due times** manifested His word through preaching, which is committed **unto me**."[146]

Clearly God had new information to reveal through Paul. The risen Christ appeared to Paul several times to progressively reveal the things pertaining to this new dispensation.[147]

---

[145] Ephesians 3:9.
[146] Titus 1:3.
[147] Acts 26:16; Galatians 1:11–12; 2 Corinthians 12:1–2.

Scripture Verses

Luke 1:70

As he spake by the mouth of his holy prophets, which have been since the world began.

Acts 3:24

Yea, and all the prophets from Samuel and those that follow after, as many as have spoken, have likewise foretold of these days.

Colossians 1:25–26

Whereof I am made a minister, according to the dispensation of God which is given to me for you, to fulfil the word of God;

Even the mystery which hath been hid from ages and from generations, but now is made manifest to his saints:

Romans 16:25

Now to him that is of power to stablish you according to my gospel, and the preaching of Jesus Christ, according to the revelation of the mystery, which was kept secret since the world began.

Ephesians 3:5

If ye have heard of the dispensation of the grace of God which is given me to you-ward:

How that by revelation he made known unto me the mystery; (as I wrote afore in few words,

Whereby, when ye read, ye may understand my knowledge in the mystery of Christ)

Which in other ages was not made known unto the sons of men, as it is now revealed unto his holy apostles and prophets by the Spirit.

Ephesians 3:9

And to make all men see what is the fellowship of the mystery, which from the beginning of the world hath been hid in God, who created all things by Jesus Christ.

Titus 1:3

But hath in due times manifested his word through preaching, which is committed unto me according to the commandment of God our Saviour.

Acts 26:16

But rise, and stand upon thy feet: for I have appeared unto thee for this purpose, to make thee a minister and a witness both of these things which thou hast seen, and of those things in the which I will appear unto thee.

Galatians 1:11–12

But I certify you, brethren, that the gospel which was preached of me is not after man.

For I neither received it of man, neither was I taught it, but by the revelation of Jesus Christ.

2 Corinthians 12:1–2

It is not expedient for me doubtless to glory. I will come to visions and revelations of the Lord.

I knew a man in Christ above fourteen years ago, (whether in the body, I cannot tell; or whether out of the body, I cannot tell: God knoweth;) such an one caught up to the third heaven.

THROUGH THEIR FALL
SALVATION IS COME
UNTO THE GENTILES[148]

S o what changed with the new dispensation?

The covenants and promises of the Old Testament foretold that the salvation of the Gentiles, and their subsequent blessings in the kingdom, would be through the *rise* of Israel.[149] Israel had been chosen by God to be a "kingdom of priests" and a "light to the Gentiles."[150] The gospels and early Acts focused on the fulfillment of these promises being "at hand."

However, today, in the dispensation of grace, Gentiles are not being blessed through the *rise* of Israel as prophesied but "rather through their **fall** salvation is come unto the Gentiles." Israel has been cast away (temporarily).[151] Israel is now seen by God on the same level as the Gentiles: no longer in favored nation status.

This is a drastic change from the prophesied plan!

The fulfillment of prophecy has been temporarily interrupted.

The Fall
of Israel

Jews and Gentiles on equal ground

---

148 Exodus 19:5–6; Isaiah 61:6–9; Isaiah 60.
149 Romans 11:11.
150 Romans 11:11, 15.
151 See pages 38–48.

Scripture Verses

Exodus 19:5–6

Now therefore, if ye will obey my voice indeed, and keep my covenant, then ye shall be a peculiar treasure unto me above all people: for all the earth is mine:

And ye shall be unto me a kingdom of priests, and an holy nation. These are the words which thou shalt speak unto the children of Israel.

Isaiah 61:6–9

But ye shall be named the Priests of the LORD: men shall call you the Ministers of our God: ye shall eat the riches of the Gentiles, and in their glory shall ye boast yourselves.

For your shame ye shall have double; and for confusion they shall rejoice in their portion: therefore in their land they shall possess the double: everlasting joy shall be unto them.

For I the LORD love judgment, I hate robbery for burnt offering; and I will direct their work in truth, and I will make an everlasting covenant with them.

And their seed shall be known among the Gentiles, and their offspring among the people: all that see them shall acknowledge them, that they are the seed which the LORD hath blessed.

Isaiah 60

Arise, shine; for thy light is come, and the glory of the LORD is risen upon thee.

For, behold, the darkness shall cover the earth, and gross darkness the people: but the LORD shall arise upon thee, and his glory shall be seen upon thee.

And the Gentiles shall come to thy light, and kings to the brightness of thy rising.

Lift up thine eyes round about, and see: all they gather themselves together, they come to thee: thy sons shall come from far, and thy daughters shall be nursed at thy side.

Then thou shalt see, and flow together, and thine heart shall fear, and be enlarged; because the abundance of the sea shall be converted unto thee, the forces of the Gentiles shall come unto thee.

The multitude of camels shall cover thee, the dromedaries of Midian and Ephah; all they from Sheba shall come: they shall bring gold and incense; and they shall shew forth the praises of the LORD.

All the flocks of Kedar shall be gathered together unto thee, the rams of Nebaioth shall minister unto thee: they shall come up with acceptance on mine altar, and I will glorify the house of my glory.

Who are these that fly as a cloud, and as the doves to their windows?

Surely the isles shall wait for me, and the ships of Tarshish first, to bring thy sons from far, their silver and their gold with them, unto the name of the LORD thy God, and to the Holy One of Israel, because he hath glorified thee.

And the sons of strangers shall build up thy walls, and their kings shall minister unto thee: for in my wrath I smote thee, but in my favour have I had mercy on thee.

Therefore thy gates shall be open continually; they shall not be shut day nor night; that men may bring unto thee the forces of the Gentiles, and that their kings may be brought.

For the nation and kingdom that will not serve thee shall perish; yea, those nations shall be utterly wasted.

The glory of Lebanon shall come unto thee, the fir tree, the pine tree, and the box together, to beautify the place of my sanctuary; and I will make the place of my feet glorious.

The sons also of them that afflicted thee shall come bending unto thee; and all they that despised thee shall bow themselves down at the soles of thy feet; and they shall call thee; The city of the LORD, The Zion of the Holy One of Israel.

Whereas thou has been forsaken and hated, so that no man went through thee, I will make thee an eternal excellency, a joy of many generations.

Thou shalt also suck the milk of the Gentiles, and shalt suck the breast of kings: and thou shalt know that I the LORD am thy Saviour and thy Redeemer, the mighty One of Jacob.

For brass I will bring gold, and for iron I will bring silver, and for wood brass, and for stones iron: I will also make thy officers peace, and thine exactors righteousness.

Violence shall no more be heard in thy land, wasting nor destruction within thy borders; but thou shalt call thy walls Salvation, and thy gates Praise.

The sun shall be no more thy light by day; neither for brightness shall the moon give light unto thee: but the LORD shall be unto thee an everlasting light, and thy God thy glory. Thy sun shall no more go down; neither shall thy moon withdraw itself: for the LORD shall be thine everlasting light, and the days of thy mourning shall be ended.

Thy people also shall be all righteous: they shall inherit the land for ever, the branch of my planting, the work of my hands, that I may be glorified.

A little one shall become a thousand, and a small one a strong nation: I the LORD will hasten it in his time.

Romans 11:11

I say then, Have they stumbled that they should fall? God forbid: but rather through their fall salvation is come unto the Gentiles, for to provoke them to jealousy.

Romans 11:11, 15

I say then, Have they stumbled that they should fall? God forbid: but rather through their fall salvation is come unto the Gentiles, for to provoke them to jealousy.

For if the casting away of them be the reconciling of the world, what shall the receiving of them be, but life from the dead?

NOTES

A New Church: "The Body of Christ" (Middle Wall of the Partition Broken Down)

In time past, believers of Israel (and proselytes) were God's "church."[152] ("Church" simply means a called-out assembly.) They comprise the church that will inherit the kingdom of God *on earth.*[153]

According to Ephesians 2:11–12, "**in time past**" Gentiles, apart from Israel, were "without Christ, **being aliens from the commonwealth of Israel, and strangers from the covenants of promise**, having no hope, and without God in the world."

"**But now** in Christ Jesus ye who sometimes were far off are made nigh by the blood of Christ" (Eph. 2:13). Through Paul's epistles, God says He has "broken down the middle wall of partition [page 20]...to make in Himself of twain [Jew and Gentile] **one new man**...that He might reconcile both unto God in **one body** [the body of Christ] by the cross."[154]

The church God is forming today is "the body of Christ."[155] It is a new body of believers not talked about in the Old Testament or the gospels. In the body of Christ, there is no difference between Jew and Gentile.[156] Today *anyone* who believes the gospel of the grace of

---

152 Matthew 18:16–18; Acts 2:47 and 7:38.
153 Luke 12:32; see page 57.
154 Ephesians 2:14–16.
155 1 Corinthians 12:27.
156 Romans 10:12.

God (page 102) becomes part of the body of Christ, not Israel. Paul says, "For by one spirit are we all baptized into one body, whether we be Jews or Gentiles."[157]

The body of Christ is separate and distinct from Israel, with its own purpose, calling, and hope.

---

[157] 1 Corinthians 12:13.

Scripture Verses

Matthew 18:16–18

But if he will not hear thee, then take with thee one or two more, that in the mouth of two or three witnesses every word may be established.

And if he shall neglect to hear them, tell it unto the church: but if he neglect to hear the church, let him be unto thee as an heathen man and a publican.

Verily I say unto you, Whatsoever ye shall bind on earth shall be bound in heaven: and whatsoever ye shall loose on earth shall be loosed in heaven.

Acts 2:47

Praising God, and having favour with all the people. And the Lord added to the church daily such as should be saved.

Acts 7:38

This is he, that was in the church in the wilderness with the angel which spake to him in the mount Sina, and with our fathers: who received the lively oracles to give unto us.

Luke 12:32

Fear not, little flock; for it is your Father's good pleasure to give you the kingdom.

Ephesians 2:14–16

For he is our peace, who hath made both one, and hath broken down the middle wall of partition between us;

Having abolished in his flesh the enmity, even the law of commandments contained in ordinances; for to make in himself of twain one new man, so making peace;

And that he might reconcile both unto God in one body by the cross, having slain the enmity thereby.

1 Corinthians 12:27

Now ye are the body of Christ, and members in particular.

Romans 10:12

For there is no difference between the Jew and the Greek: for the same Lord over all is rich unto all that call upon him.

1 Corinthians 12:13

For by one Spirit are we all baptized into one body, whether we be Jews or Gentiles, whether we be bond or free; and have been all made to drink into one Spirit.

NOTES

A NEW APOSTLE

I n the gospels, Christ chose twelve apostles to rule with Him over the twelve tribes of Israel in His kingdom. When Judas fell, the apostles chose Matthias to take his place.[158] Their number was complete, so *why Paul?*

Paul's ministry is separate from that of the twelve. God used Paul to reveal "the dispensation of the grace of God" to the Gentiles.[159] Paul, in Romans 11:13, says, "I am the apostle of the Gentiles, I magnify mine office." The risen Lord appeared to Paul several times during his ministry and progressively revealed the truths *specifically about and for the church of today, the Body of Christ, in the dispensation of grace.*[160] Note what He claims:

> According to the grace of God which is given unto me, as a wise masterbuilder, I have laid the foundation...let every man take heed how he buildeth thereupon. (1 Corinthians 3:10)
>
> For **his body's sake**, which is the **church: Whereof I am made a minister, according to the dispensation of God which is given to me** for you. (Col. 1:24–25; see also Eph. 3:1–3)
>
> Now to him that is of power to stablish you according to **my gospel**, and the preaching of Jesus Christ **according to the revelation of the mystery**, which was kept secret since the world began. (Rom. 16:25)

---

[158] Matthew 19:28; Isaiah 1:26; Acts 1:26.
[159] Ephesians 3:1–3.
[160]

Be ye followers of **me**. (1 Cor. 4:16 and 11:1)

That **in me** FIRST...for a pattern to them which should hereafter believe on him to life everlasting. (1 Tim. 1:16)

Scripture Verses

Matthew 19:28

And Jesus said unto them, Verily I say unto you, That ye which have followed me, in the regeneration when the Son of man shall sit in the throne of his glory, ye also shall sit upon twelve thrones, judging the twelve tribes of Israel.

Isaiah 1:26

And I will restore thy judges as at the first, and thy counsellors as at the beginning: afterward thou shalt be called, The city of righteousness, the faithful city.

Acts 1:26

And they gave forth their lots; and the lot fell upon Matthias; and he was numbered with the eleven apostles.

Ephesians 3:1–3

For this cause I Paul, the prisoner of Jesus Christ for you Gentiles,

If ye have heard of the dispensation of the grace of God which is given me to you-ward:

How that by revelation he made known unto me the mystery; (as I wrote afore in few words).

NOTES

FROM LAW TO GRACE

During His earthly ministry, Christ taught the law (see page 67). *Believing* Jews in Acts who were saved under the kingdom gospel continued to keep the law. (See Acts 10:14 and 21:20. Also, Hebrews 8:13, written in the Acts time frame, says the old covenant "is ***ready*** *to vanish away.*")

But through the apostle Paul, the *risen* Christ revealed "the end of the law" (Rom. 10:4) and salvation by grace through faith *in the shed blood of Christ alone*, apart from the law and apart from works. In Romans 3:21–28 Paul says this:

> **But now** the righteousness of God **without the law** is manifested… Even the righteousness of God *which* is by faith of Jesus Christ unto all and upon all them that believe… Being justified freely by His grace through the redemption that is in Christ Jesus: Whom God hath set forth *to be* a propitiation **through faith in His blood**…a man is justified by faith **without the deeds of the law**.

It is in Paul's epistles that we read things like the following:

> For ye are not under the law, but under grace. (Rom. 6:14)

> To him that **worketh not**, but believeth on him that justifieth the ungodly, his faith is counted for righteousness. (Rom. 4:5)

In him, not having mine own righteousness, which is of the law, but that which is through the faith of Christ, the righteousness which is of God by faith. (Phil. 3:9)

For **by grace** are ye saved through faith; and that not of yourselves: *it is* the gift of God: **Not of works**. (Eph. 2:8–9)

Stand fast therefore in the liberty wherewith Christ hath made us free, and be not entangled again with the yoke of bondage. (Gal. 5:1)

THE PREACHING
OF THE CROSS

While the Old Testament and the gospels did reveal that Christ would die and be raised for the sins of *His people* (Israel),[161] the shed blood of Christ was not at the heart of "the gospel of the kingdom" preached during the earthly ministry of Christ and early Acts.

To "believe on Christ" at that time was to believe that He was the Son of God, the promised Christ and King of Israel.[162] As late as Luke 18:31–34, after extensively preaching their gospel, the apostles did not even understand that Christ would have to die. (See page 74.) After His death, they did not preach the cross as good news to rest in but as a wicked deed that Israel needed to repent of.[163]

This is because there are many things that the cross of Christ accomplished that God purposely kept hidden until He revealed them through Paul. He kept this "hidden wisdom" a secret so that Satan and his princes would not know it, **"for had they known *it*, they would not have crucified the Lord of glory."**[164]

The "hidden wisdom" about the cross is at the heart of the gospel of the grace of God and the mystery revealed through Paul. "The preaching of the cross," as Paul calls it, is what makes salvation by grace *through faith in the blood of*

---

[161] Isaiah 53:8,12; Acts 5:31.
[162] John 1:49; Matthew 16:16; John 20:30–31.
[163] Acts 2:22–24 and 32–38.
[164] 1 Corinthians 2:7–8.

Christ alone possible. Paul says, "Unto us which are saved, it is the power of God."[165] The preaching of the cross begins with the good news that Christ "was delivered **for our offenses**, and was raised again **for our justification**,"[166] but it is so much more. It is everything that God is free to do because of the sacrifice of Christ.

A critical fact to note: In Matthew 26:28, Christ says that His blood "is shed **for many**" (meaning Israel). But Paul declares that Christ "gave himself a ransom **for all**, to be testified **in due time**. Whereunto I am ordained a preacher, and an apostle" (1 Tim. 2:6–7).

---

[165] 1 Corinthians 1:18.
[166] Romans 4:25; 1 Corinthians 15:3–4.

Scripture Verses

Isaiah 53:8, 12

He was taken from prison and from judgment: and who shall declare his generation? for he was cut off out of the land of the living: for the transgression of my people was he stricken.

Therefore will I divide him a portion with the great, and he shall divide the spoil with the strong; because he hath poured out his soul unto death: and he was numbered with the transgressors; and he bare the sin of many, and made intercession for the transgressors.

Acts 5:31

Him hath God exalted with his right hand to be a Prince and a Saviour, for to give repentance to Israel, and forgiveness of sins.

John 1:49

Nathanael answered and saith unto him, Rabbi, thou art the Son of God; thou art the King of Israel.

Matthew 16:16

And Simon Peter answered and said, Thou art the Christ, the Son of the living God.

John 20:30–31

And many other signs truly did Jesus in the presence of his disciples, which are not written in this book:

But these are written, that ye might believe that Jesus is the Christ, the Son of God; and that believing ye might have life through his name.

Acts 2:22–24

Ye men of Israel, hear these words; Jesus of Nazareth, a man approved of God among you by miracles and wonders and signs, which God did by him in the midst of you, as ye yourselves also know:

Him, being delivered by the determinate counsel and foreknowledge of God, ye have taken, and by wicked hands have crucified and slain:

Whom God hath raised up, having loosed the pains of death: because it was not possible that he should be holden of it.

Acts 2:32–38

This Jesus hath God raised up, whereof we all are witnesses.

Therefore being by the right hand of God exalted, and having received of the Father the promise of the Holy Ghost, he hath shed forth this, which ye now see and hear.

For David is not ascended into the heavens: but he saith himself, The Lord said unto my Lord, Sit thou on my right hand,

Until I make thy foes thy footstool.

Therefore let all the house of Israel know assuredly, that God hath made the same Jesus, whom ye have crucified, both Lord and Christ.

Now when they heard this, they were pricked in their heart, and said unto Peter and to the rest of the apostles, Men and brethren, what shall we do?

Then Peter said unto them, Repent, and be baptized every one of you in the name of Jesus Christ for the remission of sins, and ye shall receive the gift of the Holy Ghost.

1 Corinthians 2:7–8

But we speak the wisdom of God in a mystery, even the hidden wisdom, which God ordained before the world unto our glory:

Which none of the princes of this world knew: for had they known it, they would not have crucified the Lord of glory.

1 Corinthians 1:18

For Christ sent me not to baptize, but to preach the gospel: not with wisdom of words, lest the cross of Christ should be made of none effect.

For the preaching of the cross is to them that perish foolishness; but unto us which are saved it is the power of God.

Romans 4:25

But to him that worketh not, but believeth on him that justifieth the ungodly, his faith is counted for righteousness.

1 Corinthians 15:3–4

For I delivered unto you first of all that which I also received, how that Christ died for our sins according to the scriptures; And that he was buried, and that he rose again the third day according to the scriptures.

NOTES

COMPLETE IN CHRIST

One of the most blessed truths we learn through "the preaching of the cross" is our completeness *in Christ.*[167]

During this dispensation of grace, the moment a person places his faith in the shed blood of Christ *alone* for salvation, he is "baptized **into Jesus Christ**" by the Holy Spirit[168]—into His death, burial, and resurrection.[169] Believers are "sealed with that Holy Spirit of promise."[170] *In Christ,* believers have complete forgiveness of all their sins and the imputed righteousness of God—the righteousness of God which is by faith of Jesus Christ.[171] We become "heirs of God, and joint-heirs with Christ,"[172] and nothing "shall be able to separate us from the love of God, which is **in Christ Jesus our Lord**." [173]

---

[167]   Colossians 2:10.
[168]   Romans 6:3; 1 Corinthians 12:13.
[169]   Romans 6:3–8; Galatians 2:20.
[170]   Ephesians 1:13–14.
[171]   2 Corinthians 5:21; Philippians 3:9; Ephesians1:7.
[172]   Romans 8:17.
[173]   Romans 8:35–39.

This is a contrast to Israel's program in time past. Today, *in Christ*, among the many blessings we have, we also have spiritually what was required of Israel physically under the law:

- Israel had to continually offer blood sacrifices for sins; we now know we have total, complete forgiveness of all our sins—past, present, and future—by the blood of Christ.[174]
- Israel had to be physically circumcised; we are spiritually circumcised "with the circumcision made without hands… **by the circumcision of Christ**."[175]
- Israel had to be physically baptized with water; we are "buried **with Him in baptism**…through the faith of the operation of God"—a spiritual baptism into the death of Christ.[176]

---

[174] Colossians 2:13–14 and 1:14; Romans 3:25; Ephesians 1:7.
[175] Colossians 2:11.
[176] Colossians 2:12; Romans 6:3–12; 1 Corinthians 12:13; Galatians 3:27.

Scripture Verses

Colossians 2:10

And ye are complete in him, which is the head of all principality and power.

Romans 6:3

Know ye not, that so many of us as were baptized into Jesus Christ were baptized into his death?

1 Corinthians 12:13

For by one Spirit are we all baptized into one body, whether we be Jews or Gentiles, whether we be bond or free; and have been all made to drink into one Spirit.

Romans 6:3–8

Know ye not, that so many of us as were baptized into Jesus Christ were baptized into his death?

Therefore we are buried with him by baptism into death: that like as Christ was raised up from the dead by the glory of the Father, even so we also should walk in newness of life.

For if we have been planted together in the likeness of his death, we shall be also in the likeness of his resurrection:

Knowing this, that our old man is crucified with him, that the body of sin might be destroyed, that henceforth we should not serve sin.

For he that is dead is freed from sin. 8 Now if we be dead with Christ, we believe that we shall also live with him.

Galatians 2:20

I am crucified with Christ: nevertheless I live; yet not I, but Christ liveth in me: and the life which I now live in the flesh I live by the faith of the Son of God, who loved me, and gave himself for me.

Ephesians 1:13–14

In whom ye also trusted, after that ye heard the word of truth, the gospel of your salvation: in whom also after that ye believed, ye were sealed with that holy Spirit of promise,

14 Which is the earnest of our inheritance until the redemption of the purchased possession, unto the praise of his glory.

2 Corinthians 5:21

For he hath made him to be sin for us, who knew no sin; that we might be made the righteousness of God in him.

Philippians 3:9

And be found in him, not having mine own righteousness, which is of the law, but that which is through the faith of Christ, the righteousness which is of God by faith:

Ephesians 1:7

In whom we have redemption through his blood, the forgiveness of sins, according to the riches of his grace.

Romans 8:17

And if children, then heirs; heirs of God, and joint-heirs with Christ; if so be that we suffer with him, that we may be also glorified together.

Romans 8:35–39

Who shall separate us from the love of Christ? shall tribulation, or distress, or persecution, or famine, or nakedness, or peril, or sword?

As it is written, For thy sake we are killed all the day long; we are accounted as sheep for the slaughter.

Nay, in all these things we are more than conquerors through him that loved us.

For I am persuaded, that neither death, nor life, nor angels, nor principalities, nor powers, nor things present, nor things to come,

Nor height, nor depth, nor any other creature, shall be able to separate us from the love of God, which is in Christ Jesus our Lord.

Colossians 2:13–14

And you, being dead in your sins and the uncircumcision of your flesh, hath he quickened together with him, having forgiven you all trespasses;

Blotting out the handwriting of ordinances that was against us, which was contrary to us, and took it out of the way, nailing it to his cross.

Colossians 1:14

In whom we have redemption through his blood, even the forgiveness of sins.

Romans 3:25

Whom God hath set forth to be a propitiation through faith in his blood, to declare his righteousness for the remission of sins that are past, through the forbearance of God.

Ephesians 1:7

In whom we have redemption through his blood, the forgiveness of sins, according to the riches of his grace.

Colossians 2:11

In whom also ye are circumcised with the circumcision made without hands, in putting off the body of the sins of the flesh by the circumcision of Christ.

Colossians 2:12

Buried with him in baptism, wherein also ye are risen with him through the faith of the operation of God, who hath raised him from the dead.

Romans 6:3–12

Know ye not, that so many of us as were baptized into Jesus Christ were baptized into his death?

Therefore we are buried with him by baptism into death: that like as Christ was raised up from the dead by the glory of the Father, even so we also should walk in newness of life.

For if we have been planted together in the likeness of his death, we shall be also in the likeness of his resurrection:

Knowing this, that our old man is crucified with him, that the body of sin might be destroyed, that henceforth we should not serve sin.

For he that is dead is freed from sin.

Now if we be dead with Christ, we believe that we shall also live with him:

Knowing that Christ being raised from the dead dieth no more; death hath no more dominion over him.

For in that he died, he died unto sin once: but in that he liveth, he liveth unto God.

Likewise reckon ye also yourselves to be dead indeed unto sin, but alive unto God through Jesus Christ our Lord.

Let not sin therefore reign in your mortal body, that ye should obey it in the lusts thereof.

1 Corinthians 12:13

For by one Spirit are we all baptized into one body, whether we be Jews or Gentiles, whether we be bond or free; and have been all made to drink into one Spirit.

Galatians 3:27

For as many of you as have been baptized into Christ have put on Christ.

NOTES

A New Commission
The Ministry of
Reconciliation

P rior to His ascension, Christ gave His apostles what has been called "The Great Commission." He instructed them that, beginning at Jerusalem, then Judea, then Samaria (the land promised to Israel), and finally all nations, they were to go and teach men "to observe all things whatsoever I have commanded you."[177]

This would mean the truths about the kingdom being at hand. It would also include the law.[178] In this commission, Christ sent them to baptize for the remission of sins. He said, "He that believeth and is baptized shall be saved," and that is what was preached in early Acts.[179]

In contrast, Paul says, "Christ sent me **not to baptize**."[180] In the revelation given to Paul, we find that believers today have a spiritual baptism that has replaced water baptism.[181] In addition, He sent Paul to preach that "Christ is the end of the law for righteousness to everyone that believeth,"[182] so that we are "not under the law, but under grace." (See page 184.) It is clear that Paul is operating under a different commission than the twelve. Indeed, to the body of Christ, God has given a new commission, found in 2 Corinthians 5:16–21, called "the ministry of reconciliation." As "ambassadors for Christ,"

---

177 Matthew 28:19+; Mark 16:15+; Luke 24:46+; Acts 1:8.
178 Matthew 28:20; 23:1–3.
179 Mark 16:16; Acts 2:38.
180 1 Corinthians 1:17.
181 1 Corinthians 12:13; Colossians 2:10–12; Romans 6; Ephesians 4:5; Galatians 3:27.
182 Romans 10:4.

we are to proclaim to the world that "God was **in Christ**, reconciling the world unto Himself, not imputing their trespasses unto them… For He [God] hath made Him [Christ] *to be* sin for us, who knew no sin; that we might be made the righteousness of God **in Him**."

Scripture Verses

Matthew 28:19

Go ye therefore, and teach all nations, baptizing them in the name of the Father, and of the Son, and of the Holy Ghost.

Mark 16:15

And he said unto them, Go ye into all the world, and preach the gospel to every creature.

Luke 24:46

And said unto them, Thus it is written, and thus it behooved Christ to suffer, and to rise from the dead the third day.

Acts 1:8

But ye shall receive power, after that the Holy Ghost is come upon you: and ye shall be witnesses unto me both in Jerusalem, and in all Judaea, and in Samaria, and unto the uttermost part of the earth.

Matthew 28:20

Teaching them to observe all things whatsoever I have commanded you: and, lo, I am with you always, even unto the end of the world. Amen.

Matthew 23:1–3

Then spake Jesus to the multitude, and to his disciples,

Saying The scribes and the Pharisees sit in Moses' seat:

All therefore whatsoever they bid you observe, that observe and do; but do not ye after their works: for they say, and do not.

Mark 16:16

He that believeth and is baptized shall be saved; but he that believeth not shall be damned.

Acts 2:38

Then Peter said unto them, Repent, and be baptized every one of you in the name of Jesus Christ for the remission of sins, and ye shall receive the gift of the Holy Ghost.

1 Corinthians 1:17

For Christ sent me not to baptize, but to preach the gospel: not with wisdom of words, lest the cross of Christ should be made of none effect.

1 Corinthians 12:13

For by one Spirit are we all baptized into one body, whether we be Jews or Gentiles, whether we be bond or free; and have been all made to drink into one Spirit.

Colossians 2:10–12

And ye are complete in him, which is the head of all principality and power:

In whom also ye are circumcised with the circumcision made without hands, in putting off the body of the sins of the flesh by the circumcision of Christ:

Buried with him in baptism, wherein also ye are risen with him through the faith of the operation of God, who hath raised him from the dead.

Romans 6

What shall we say then? Shall we continue in sin, that grace may abound?

God forbid. How shall we, that are dead to sin, live any longer therein?

Know ye not, that so many of us as were baptized into Jesus Christ were baptized into his death?

Therefore we are buried with him by baptism into death: that like as Christ was raised up from the dead by the glory of the Father, even so we also should walk in newness of life.

For if we have been planted together in the likeness of his death, we shall be also in the likeness of his resurrection:

Knowing this, that our old man is crucified with him, that the body of sin might be destroyed, that henceforth we should not serve sin.

For he that is dead is freed from sin.

Now if we be dead with Christ, we believe that we shall also live with him:

Knowing that Christ being raised from the dead dieth no more; death hath no more dominion over him.

For in that he died, he died unto sin once: but in that he liveth, he liveth unto God.

Likewise reckon ye also yourselves to be dead indeed

unto sin, but alive unto God through Jesus Christ our Lord.

Let not sin therefore reign in your mortal body, that ye should obey it in the lusts thereof.

Neither yield ye your members as instruments of unrighteousness unto sin: but yield yourselves unto God, as those that are alive from the dead, and your members as instruments of righteousness unto God.

For sin shall not have dominion over you: for ye are not under the law, but under grace.

What then? shall we sin, because we are not under the law, but under grace? God forbid.

Know ye not, that to whom ye yield yourselves servants to obey, his servants ye are to whom ye obey; whether of sin unto death, or of obedience unto righteousness?

But God be thanked, that ye were the servants of sin, but ye have obeyed from the heart that form of doctrine which was delivered you.

Being then made free from sin, ye became the servants of righteousness.

I speak after the manner of men because of the infirmity of your flesh: for as ye have yielded your members servants to uncleanness and to iniquity unto iniquity; even so now yield your members servants to righteousness unto holiness.

For when ye were the servants of sin, ye were free from righteousness.

What fruit had ye then in those things whereof ye are now ashamed? for the end of those things is death.

But now being made free from sin, and become servants to God, ye have your fruit unto holiness, and the end everlasting life.

For the wages of sin is death; but the gift of God is eternal life through Jesus Christ our Lord.

Ephesians 4:5

One Lord, one faith, one baptism.

Galatians 3:27

For as many of you as have been baptized into Christ have put on Christ.

Romans 10:4

For Christ is the end of the law for righteousness to every one that believeth.

A New Hope: Heaven

P rior to the dispensation of grace, the hope of God's people was to be resurrected into a kingdom God will establish on this earth.[183] And, indeed, those who were saved in the Old Testament and under the kingdom gospel will be resurrected into that kingdom.

Christ will one day be king over the earth.[184] He taught that He would go away *and return.*[185] He said, "The meek shall inherit **the earth**."[186] The book of Revelation looks forward to the coming of God's kingdom to this earth when new Jerusalem will descend from heaven.[187]

But in Paul's epistles, the hope of the believer is a home "**eternal in the heavens.**"[188] Members of the body of Christ will rule and reign with Christ **in the heavenly places**. In fact, Ephesians 2:6 says that God already sees us raised up together and seated together in heavenly places in Christ Jesus.

Philippians 3:20 is clear that "our conversation is in heaven," and 1 Corinthians 6:3 says we shall judge angels. Remember, God's kingdom has two realms. He will rule both heaven and earth.

The body of Christ is the agency God is going to use to reclaim the heavenly places that have been corrupted by the fallen angels.

---

[183] See pages 38, 42, and 57.
[184] Zechariah14:9; Jeremiah 33:14–17; Psalm 72:8.
[185] John 14:3; Luke 19:12 with Daniel 7:13–14.
[186] Matthew 5:5 and Psalm 37:9.
[187] Revelation 21:2, 10.
[188] 2 Corinthians 5:1.

Scripture Verses

Refer to pages 38, 42, and 57

Zechariah 14:9

And the LORD shall be king over all the earth: in that day shall there be one LORD, and his name one.

Jeremiah 33:14–17

Behold, the days come, saith the LORD, that I will perform that good thing which I have promised unto the house of Israel and to the house of Judah.

In those days, and at that time, will I cause the Branch of righteousness to grow up unto David; and he shall execute judgment and righteousness in the land.

In those days shall Judah be saved, and Jerusalem shall dwell safely: and this is the name wherewith she shall be called, The LORD our righteousness.

For thus saith the LORD; David shall never want a man to sit upon the throne of the house of Israel.

Psalms 72:8

He shall have dominion also from sea to sea, and from the river unto the ends of the earth.

John 14:3

And if I go and prepare a place for you, I will come again, and receive you unto myself; that where I am, there ye may be also.

Luke 19:12

He said therefore, A certain nobleman went into a far country to receive for himself a kingdom, and to return.

Daniel 7:13–14

I saw in the night visions, and, behold, one like the Son of man came with the clouds of heaven, and came to the Ancient of days, and they brought him near before him.

And there was given him dominion, and glory, and a kingdom, that all people, nations, and languages, should serve him: his dominion is an everlasting dominion, which shall not pass away, and his kingdom that which shall not be destroyed.

Matthew 5:5

Blessed are the meek: for they shall inherit the earth.

Psalm 37:9

For evildoers shall be cut off: but those that wait upon the LORD, they shall inherit the earth.

Revelation 21:2, 10

And I John saw the holy city, new Jerusalem, coming down from God out of heaven, prepared as a bride adorned for her husband.

And he carried me away in the spirit to a great and high mountain, and shewed me that great city, the holy Jerusalem, descending out of heaven from God.

2 Corinthians 5:1

For we know that if our earthly house of this tabernacle were dissolved, we have a building of God, an house not made with hands, eternal in the heavens.

WHY KEPT SECRET?

T hy did God keep the good news about this age of grace and the body of Christ a secret? Here, 1 Corinthians 2:7–8 gives us the answer:

> But we speak the wisdom of God in a mystery, *even* the hidden *wisdom*, which God ordained before the world unto our glory: Which none of the princes of this world knew: for **had they known *it*, they would not have crucified the Lord of glory**.

When Satan inspired the leaders of Israel to call for the crucifixion of Christ, he was gambling that this would require God to abandon His people forever;[189] thus, the earth would remain his. What he did not know was that not only was the death of Christ the means whereby God would later redeem His nation and take back the earth, it was also the means whereby He would form a new agency, the body of Christ, to reconcile the heavenly places unto Christ.

By keeping the body of Christ—the "one new man"—a secret, God was able to take Satan in his own craftiness.[190] Satan and his princes gambled for the earth, and in so doing, they lost both earth and heaven in the ages to come. By Christ's victorious work on the cross, "he made a shew of them openly, triumphing over them in it."[191]

---

[189] Satan did know that Christ was to die, but Israel was supposed to sacrifice "the lamb of God" by faith. (Compare Psalm 118:26–27 w/ Matt. 21:9.) Satan was able to inspire Israel to call for his death in unbelief, by "wicked hands" (Acts 2:23).

[190] 1 Corinthians 3:19.

[191] Colossians 2:15.

Scripture Verses

Compare Psalm 118:26–27 with Matthew 21:9; Acts 2:23

Psalm 118:26–27

Blessed be he that cometh in the name of the LORD: we have blessed you out of the house of the LORD.

God is the LORD, which hath shewed us light: bind the sacrifice with cords, even unto the horns of the altar.

Matthew 21:9

And the multitudes that went before, and that followed, cried, saying, Hosanna to the son of David: Blessed is he that cometh in the name of the Lord; Hosanna in the highest.

Acts 2:23

Him, being delivered by the determinate counsel and foreknowledge of God, ye have taken, and by wicked hands have crucified and slain.

1 Corinthians 3:19

For the wisdom of this world is foolishness with God. For it is written, He taketh the wise in their own craftiness.

Colossians 2:15

And having spoiled principalities and powers, he made a shew of them openly, triumphing over them in it.

NOTES

_____

Paul's Warning

Paul desired "to make all *men* see what *is* the fellowship of the mystery, which from the beginning of the world hath been hid in God."[192] But "the mystery"—the truths the risen Lord Jesus Christ revealed through Paul—is what Satan hates because it reveals how the cross was his defeat.

It is the "preaching of Jesus Christ, according to the revelation of the mystery,"[193] that Satan tenaciously fights to keep hidden.[194]

Paul warned that after his departure, "grievous wolves" would enter in and "of your own selves shall men arise, speaking perverse things, to draw away disciples."[195] Even before he died, Paul had to say, "All they which are in Asia be turned away *from me*."[196] The majority of the churches he had started had left his doctrine, most returning to the law. (This is one reason that we cannot rely on "the church fathers" for our doctrine. We must rely on the word of God alone.)

Even to this day, many still fail to see Paul's distinctive ministry and understand "the mystery" God revealed through him. This is sad because Paul said that it is "**my** gospel and the preaching of Jesus Christ, **according to the revelation of the mystery**" that God uses to "stablish" a believer in this dispensation.[197]

It is no wonder that the church is in such confusion today.

---

192 Ephesians 3:9.
193 Romans 16:25.
194 2 Corinthians 4:3–4.
195 Acts 20:29–30.
196 2 Timothy 1:15.
197 Romans 16:25.

Scripture Verses

Ephesians 3:9

And to make all men see what is the fellowship of the mystery, which from the beginning of the world hath been hid in God, who created all things by Jesus Christ.

Romans 16:25

Now to him that is of power to stablish you according to my gospel, and the preaching of Jesus Christ, according to the revelation of the mystery, which was kept secret since the world began.

2 Corinthians 4:3–4

But if our gospel be hid, it is hid to them that are lost:

4 In whom the god of this world hath blinded the minds of them which believe not, lest the light of the glorious gospel of Christ, who is the image of God, should shine unto them.

Acts 20:29–30

Wolves enter in among you, not sparing the flock.

Also of your own selves shall men arise, speaking perverse things, to draw away disciples after them.

2 Timothy 1:15

That good thing which was committed unto thee keep by the Holy Ghost which dwelleth in us.

Romans 16:25

Now to him that is of power to stablish you according to my gospel, and the preaching of Jesus Christ, according to the revelation of the mystery, which was kept secret since the world began.

NOTES

SOLVING THE CONFUSION

ailing to recognize the distinctiveness of "the revelation of the mystery" given to Paul by the *risen* Christ leads to confusion, even with respect to something as basic and important as the gospel. This is because mixing the kingdom gospel with the gospel of the grace of God perverts the gospel for today.

When Christ and the twelve preached the kingdom gospel, the law was still in effect. Christ said, "Whosoever shall do and teach the same [the commandments of the law], shall be called great in the kingdom of heaven."[198] Also, Christ and the twelve commanded various works. For example, Christ said, "He that believeth **and is baptized** shall be saved,"[199] and, "Sell that ye have."[200] Peter preached, "Repent and **be baptized...for the remission of sins**."[201] These are *not* the gospel of the grace of God for today.

In addition, Christians who try to apply verses given to Israel living under the law (or in the tribulation period) to today often doubt their eternal security. Verses such as the following cause them to question their security in Christ:

> He that shall endure to the end, the same shall be saved. (Matt. 24:13)
> For it is impossible for those who were once enlightened... If they shall fall away, to renew them again unto repentance. (Heb. 6:4–6)

---

[198]   Matthew 5:17; see also Matthew 23:21, 8:4; Luke 5:14.
[199]   Mark 16:16.
[200]   Luke 12:33.
[201]   Acts 2:38.

> Ask and it will be given to you; seek and you
> will find; knock, and it will be opened to you.
> (Matt. 7:7)

These verses mean what they say for the time and situation in which they were said. However, they do not apply today. In this age of grace, *no works of any kind are required for salvation* and *all believers are eternally secure*. It is *through* Paul that God explains how we are justified apart from the law and works:

> Being **justified freely by his grace** through
> the redemption that is in Christ Jesus: Whom
> God hath set forth to be a propitiation **through
> faith in his blood**. (Rom. 3:24–25; see pages
> 102–109)

Scripture Verses

Matthew 5:17

Think not that I am come to destroy the law, or the prophets: I am not come to destroy, but to fulfil.

Matthew 23:21

And whoso shall swear by the temple, sweareth by it, and by him that dwelleth therein.

Matthew 8:4

And Jesus saith unto him, See thou tell no man; but go thy way, shew thyself to the priest, and offer the gift that Moses commanded, for a testimony unto them.

Luke 5:14

And he charged him to tell no man: but go, and shew thyself to the priest, and offer for thy cleansing, according as Moses commanded, for a testimony unto them.

Mark 16:16

He that believeth and is baptized shall be saved; but he that believeth not shall be damned.

And these signs shall follow them that believe; In my name shall they cast out devils; they shall speak with new tongues;

They shall take up serpents; and if they drink any deadly thing, it shall not hurt them; they shall lay hands on the sick, and they shall recover.

Luke 12:33

Sell that ye have, and give alms; provide yourselves bags which wax not old, a treasure in the heavens that faileth not, where no thief approacheth, neither moth corrupteth.

Acts 2:38

Then Peter said unto them, Repent, and be baptized every one of you in the name of Jesus Christ for the remission of sins, and ye shall receive the gift of the Holy Ghost.

NOTES

SOLVING THE CONFUSION, CONTINUED

nother area of confusion among Christians concerns signs, wonders, and miraculous healings. In the gospels and Acts, these were a foretaste of the kingdom and validated the message that the kingdom was then at hand.[202] However, today the kingdom is not at hand. And today, the outer man is not the focus of God's activity. Instead, God is doing something far more wonderful and eternal than temporary healing and outward signs: He is working in the inner man of the believer, strengthening him by His spirit to be able to glorify him in any circumstance.[203] Even Paul, who at the beginning of his ministry had performed many signs and healings, was unable to do so by the end of his ministry.[204] But he said, "I have learned, in whatsoever state I am, *therewith* to be content" (Phil. 4:11).

Today, believers are blessed with "all **spiritual** blessings in heavenly *places* **in Christ**."[205] We understand that "though our outward man perish, yet the inward man is renewed day by day."[206] In 2 Corinthians 12:9–10, Paul explains:

> And He said unto me, **My grace is sufficient for thee:** for my strength is made perfect in weakness. Most gladly therefore will I rather

---

[202] Hebrews 2:3–4; Matthew 11:3–6 with Isaiah 35; Luke 11:20.

[203] 2 Corinthians 4:16–18; Philippians 4:11–13.

[204] 2 Corinthians 12:8–10; 2 Timothy 4:20; 1 Timothy 5:23.

[205] Ephesians 1:3.

[206] 2 Corinthians 4:16.

glory in my infirmities, that the power of Christ may rest upon me. Therefore I take pleasure in infirmities, in reproaches, in necessities, in persecutions, in distresses for Christ's sake: for when I am weak, then am I strong.

And God would have us, too, learn to rest in the sufficiency of His wonderful grace, no matter what our outward circumstances!

For our light affliction, which is but for a moment, worketh for us a far more exceeding and eternal weight of glory...for the things which are seen are temporal, but the things which are not seen are eternal.[207]

---

[207] 2 Corinthians 17–18

Scripture Verses

Hebrews 2:3–4

How shall we escape, if we neglect so great salvation; which at the first began to be spoken by the Lord, and was confirmed unto us by them that heard him;

God also bearing them witness, both with signs and wonders, and with divers miracles, and gifts of the Holy Ghost, according to his own will?

Matthew 11:3–6

And said unto him, Art thou he that should come, or do we look for another?

Jesus answered and said unto them, Go and shew John again those things which ye do hear and see:

The blind receive their sight, and the lame walk, the lepers are cleansed, and the deaf hear, the dead are raised up, and the poor have the gospel preached to them.

And blessed is he, whosoever shall not be offended in me.

Isaiah 35

The wilderness and the solitary place shall be glad for them; and the desert shall rejoice, and blossom as the rose.

It shall blossom abundantly, and rejoice even with joy and singing: the glory of Lebanon shall be given unto it, the excellency of Carmel and Sharon, they shall see the glory of the Lord, and the excellency of our God.

Strengthen ye the weak hands, and confirm the feeble knees.

Say to them that are of a fearful heart, Be strong, fear not: behold, your God will come with vengeance, even God with a recompence; he will come and save you.

Then the eyes of the blind shall be opened, and the ears of the deaf shall be unstopped.

Then shall the lame man leap as an hart, and the tongue of the dumb sing: for in the wilderness shall waters break out, and streams in the desert.

And the parched ground shall become a pool, and the thirsty land springs of water: in the habitation of dragons, where each lay, shall be grass with reeds and rushes.

And an highway shall be there, and a way, and it shall be called The way of holiness; the unclean shall not pass over it; but it shall be for those: the wayfaring men, though fools, shall not err therein.

No lion shall be there, nor any ravenous beast shall go up thereon, it shall not be found there; but the redeemed shall walk there:

And the ransomed of the Lord shall return, and come to Zion with songs and everlasting joy upon their heads: they shall obtain joy and gladness, and sorrow and sighing shall flee away.

Luke 11:20

But if I with the finger of God cast out devils, no doubt the kingdom of God is come upon you.

2 Corinthians 4:16–18

But we have this treasure in earthen vessels, that the excellency of the power may be of God, and not of us.

We are troubled on every side, yet not distressed; we are perplexed, but not in despair;

Persecuted, but not forsaken; cast down, but not destroyed;

Always bearing about in the body the dying of the Lord Jesus, that the life also of Jesus might be made manifest in our body.

Philippians 4:11–13

Not that I speak in respect of want: for I have learned, in whatsoever state I am, therewith to be content.

I know both how to be abased, and I know how to abound: every where and in all things I am instructed both to be full and to be hungry, both to abound and to suffer need.

I can do all things through Christ which strengtheneth me.

2 Corinthians 12:8–10

For this thing I besought the Lord thrice, that it might depart from me.

And he said unto me, My grace is sufficient for thee: for my strength is made perfect in weakness. Most gladly therefore will I rather glory in my infirmities, that the power of Christ may rest upon me.

Therefore I take pleasure in infirmities, in reproaches, in necessities, in persecutions, in distresses for Christ's sake: for when I am weak, then am I strong.

2 Timothy 4:20

Erastus abode at Corinth: but Trophimus have I left at Miletum sick.

1 Timothy 5:23

Drink no longer water, but use a little wine for thy stomach's sake and thine often infirmities.

Ephesians 1:3

Blessed be the God and Father of our Lord Jesus Christ, who hath blessed us with all spiritual blessings in heavenly places in Christ:

2 Corinthians 4:7–18

But we have this treasure in earthen vessels, that the excellency of the power may be of God, and not of us.

We are troubled on every side, yet not distressed; we are perplexed, but not in despair;

Persecuted, but not forsaken; cast down, but not destroyed;

Always bearing about in the body the dying of the Lord Jesus, that the life also of Jesus might be made manifest in our body.

For we which live are always delivered unto death for Jesus' sake, that the life also of Jesus might be made manifest in our mortal flesh.

So then death worketh in us, but life in you.

We having the same spirit of faith, according as it is written, I believed, and therefore have I spoken; we also believe, and therefore speak;

Knowing that he which raised up the Lord Jesus shall raise up us also by Jesus, and shall present us with you.

For all things are for your sakes, that the abundant grace might through the thanksgiving of many redound to the glory of God.

For which cause we faint not; but though our outward man perish, yet the inward man is renewed day by day.

For our light affliction, which is but for a moment, worketh for us a far more exceeding and eternal weight of glory;

While we look not at the things which are seen, but at the things which are not seen: for the things which are seen are temporal; but the things which are not seen are eternal.

NOTES

SOLVING THE CONFUSION, CONTINUED

When the Bible is not rightly divided, understanding the will of God also becomes confusing. In time past, under the law, God gave Israel detailed instructions about every aspect of their lives. The law is likened to "tutors and governors"; Israel, under the law, is likened to children and servants.[208] When Israel disobeyed, they were chastised. When they obeyed, they were blessed. External signs told them whether or not they were in the will of God.[209]

Today, however, God deals with believers as adult sons who no longer need tutors and governors.[210] We do not need external signs to determine if we are in the will of God. God has given us the indwelling Holy Spirit and His complete Word to instruct us.[211] Walking in the will of God today is simply walking in line with what God is doing today—letting Christ *in you* live out of you, and letting His word effectually work in you as you believe it and rely on it.[212]

In some areas of life, God's Word gives specific instructions. When we obey these instructions by faith, we are doing the will of God. For example, husbands are instructed to love their wives, wives to submit to their husbands, and children to obey their parents.[213] But there are many areas about which the Bible is silent. In these areas, God gives the believer, as an adult son, freedom to choose.

[208] Galatians 4:1–2.
[209] Leviticus 26.
[210] Galatians 4:4–7.
[211] Romans 8:14; Colossians 3:16.
[212] Galatians 2:20; 1 Thessalonians 2:13.
[213] Ephesians 5:21–6:1.

God does not reveal His will today by external signs. God is not *giving extra-biblical revelations.* His word is complete, making "the man of God...thoroughly furnished unto all good works."[214] We discern His will by "the renewing of [our] minds" in the Word of God.[215] As long as a decision is not contrary to sound doctrine for this dispensation of grace, a believer is free to make it without fear of being out of the will of God.

Understanding how God is working today is exciting and liberating! We do not have to wonder what God is trying to tell us—we have His complete word!

---

[214] 2 Timothy 3:16.
[215] Romans 12:1–2.

Scripture Verses

Galatians 4:1–2

Now I say, That the heir, as long as he is a child, differeth nothing from a servant, though he be lord of all;

But is under tutors and governors until the time appointed of the father.

Leviticus 26

Ye shall make you no idols nor graven image, neither rear you up a standing image, neither shall ye set up any image of stone in your land, to bow down unto it: for I am the LORD your God.

Ye shall keep my sabbaths, and reverence my sanctuary: I am the LORD.

If ye walk in my statutes, and keep my commandments, and do them;

Then I will give you rain in due season, and the land shall yield her increase, and the trees of the field shall yield their fruit.

And your threshing shall reach unto the vintage, and the vintage shall reach unto the sowing time: and ye shall eat your bread to the full, and dwell in your land safely.

And I will give peace in the land, and ye shall lie down, and none shall make you afraid: and I will rid evil beasts out of the land, neither shall the sword go through your land.

And ye shall chase your enemies, and they shall fall before you by the sword.

And five of you shall chase an hundred, and an hundred of you shall put ten thousand to flight: and your enemies shall fall before you by the sword.

For I will have respect unto you, and make you fruitful, and multiply you, and establish my covenant with you.

And ye shall eat old store, and bring forth the old because of the new.

And I set my tabernacle among you: and my soul shall not abhor you.

And I will walk among you, and will be your God, and ye shall be my people.

I am the LORD your God, which brought you forth out of the land of Egypt, that ye should not be their bondmen; and I have broken the bands of your yoke, and made you go upright.

But if ye will not hearken unto me, and will not do all these commandments;

And if ye shall despise my statutes, or if your soul abhor my judgments, so that ye will not do all my commandments, but that ye break my covenant:

I also will do this unto you; I will even appoint over you terror, consumption, and the burning ague, that shall consume the eyes, and cause sorrow of heart: and ye shall sow your seed in vain, for your enemies shall eat it.

And I will set my face against you, and ye shall be slain before your enemies: they that hate you shall reign over you; and ye shall flee when none pursueth you.

And if ye will not yet for all this hearken unto me, then I will punish you seven times more for your sins.

And I will break the pride of your power; and I will make your heaven as iron, and your earth as brass:

And your strength shall be spent in vain: for your land shall not yield her increase, neither shall the trees of the land yield their fruits.

And if ye walk contrary unto me, and will not hearken unto me; I will bring seven times more plagues upon you according to your sins.

I will also send wild beasts among you, which shall rob you of your children, and destroy your cattle, and make you few in number; and your high ways shall be desolate.

And if ye will not be reformed by me by these things, but will walk contrary unto me;

Then will I also walk contrary unto you, and will punish you yet seven times for your sins.

And I will bring a sword upon you, that shall avenge the quarrel of my covenant: and when ye are gathered together within your cities, I will send the pestilence among you; and ye shall be delivered into the hand of the enemy.

And when I have broken the staff of your bread, ten women shall bake your bread in one oven, and they shall deliver you your bread again by weight: and ye shall eat, and not be satisfied.

And if ye will not for all this hearken unto me, but walk contrary unto me;

Then I will walk contrary unto you also in fury; and I, even I, will chastise you seven times for your sins.

And ye shall eat the flesh of your sons, and the flesh of your daughters shall ye eat.

And I will destroy your high places, and cut down your images, and cast your carcases upon the carcases of your idols, and my soul shall abhor you.

And I will make your cities waste, and bring your sanctuaries unto desolation, and I will not smell the savour of your sweet odours.

And I will bring the land into desolation: and your enemies which dwell therein shall be astonished at it.

And I will scatter you among the heathen, and will draw out a sword after you: and your land shall be desolate, and your cities waste.

Then shall the land enjoy her sabbaths, as long as it lieth desolate, and ye be in your enemies' land; even then shall the land rest, and enjoy her sabbaths.

As long as it lieth desolate it shall rest; because it did not rest in your sabbaths, when ye dwelt upon it.

And upon them that are left alive of you I will send a faintness into their hearts in the lands of their enemies; and the sound of a shaken leaf shall chase them; and they shall flee, as fleeing from a sword; and they shall fall when none pursueth.

And they shall fall one upon another, as it were before a sword, when none pursueth: and ye shall have no power to stand before your enemies.

And ye shall perish among the heathen, and the land of your enemies shall eat you up.

And they that are left of you shall pine away in their iniquity in your enemies' lands; and also in the iniquities of their fathers shall they pine away with them.

If they shall confess their iniquity, and the iniquity of their fathers, with their trespass which they trespassed against me, and that also they have walked contrary unto me;

And that I also have walked contrary unto them, and have brought them into the land of their enemies; if then their uncircumcised hearts be humbled, and they then accept of the punishment of their iniquity:

Then will I remember my covenant with Jacob, and also my covenant with Isaac, and also my covenant with Abraham will I remember; and I will remember the land.

The land also shall be left of them, and shall enjoy her sabbaths, while she lieth desolate without them: and they shall accept of the punishment of their iniquity: because, even because they despised my judgments, and because their soul abhorred my statutes.

And yet for all that, when they be in the land of their enemies, I will not cast them away, neither will I abhor them, to destroy them utterly, and to break my covenant with them: for I am the LORD their God.

But I will for their sakes remember the covenant of their ancestors, whom I brought forth out of the land of Egypt in the sight of the heathen, that I might be their God: I am the LORD.

These are the statutes and judgments and laws, which the LORD made between him and the children of Israel in mount Sinai by the hand of Moses.

Galatians 4:4–7

But when the fulness of the time was come, God sent forth his Son, made of a woman, made under the law,

To redeem them that were under the law, that we might receive the adoption of sons.

And because ye are sons, God hath sent forth the Spirit of his Son into your hearts, crying, Abba, Father.

Wherefore thou art no more a servant, but a son; and if a son, then an heir of God through Christ.

Romans 8:14

For as many as are led by the Spirit of God, they are the sons of God.

Colossians 3:16

Let the word of Christ dwell in you richly in all wisdom; teaching and admonishing one another in psalms and hymns and spiritual songs, singing with grace in your hearts to the Lord.

Galatians 2:20

I am crucified with Christ: nevertheless I live; yet not I, but Christ liveth in me: and the life which I now live in the flesh I live by the faith of the Son of God, who loved me, and gave himself for me.

1 Thessalonians 2:13

For this cause also thank we God without ceasing, because, when ye received the word of God which ye heard of us, ye received it not as the word of men, but as it is in truth, the word of God, which effectually worketh also in you that believe.

Ephesians 5:21

Submitting yourselves one to another in the fear of God.

Ephesians 6:1

Children, obey your parents in the Lord: for this is right.

2 Timothy 3:16

All scripture is given by inspiration of God, and is profitable for doctrine, for reproof, for correction, for instruction in righteousness.

Romans 12:1–2

I beseech you therefore, brethren, by the mercies of God, that ye present your bodies a living sacrifice, holy, acceptable unto God, which is your reasonable service.

And be not conformed to this world: but be ye transformed by the renewing of your mind, that ye may prove what is that good, and acceptable, and perfect, will of God.

NOTES

THE END OF THE DISPENSATION

This age of grace will not last forever. It will end when Jesus Christ comes to take the members of the body of Christ—everyone saved during this dispensation of grace—to heaven, where they will rule over the angels and glorify God forever.[216]

This event is often called the rapture of the church; however, the word *rapture* is not the biblical term. In 1 Thessalonians 4:17, it says believers will be "caught up together with them [the dead in Christ] in the clouds, to meet the Lord in the air: and so shall we ever be with the Lord."

At this event, the members of the body of Christ will receive glorified bodies and be manifested to be "the sons of God." This is what the Bible calls "the adoption" of the body of Christ that we, and all of creation, are waiting for.[217]

The body of Christ will fill the heavenly places and rule and reign with Christ there forever. We will be "the fulness of Him that filleth all in all."[218] God will put us on display in the heavenly places for all of creation to see in order to show "the exceeding riches of His grace in *His* kindness toward us through Christ Jesus."[219]

This is God's "eternal purpose which he purposed in Christ Jesus our Lord"[220] for the church, the body of Christ.[221]

---

[216] 1 Thessalonians 4:16–17; 1 Corinthians 6:3.
[217] Romans 8:19–23.
[218] Ephesians 1:23.
[219] Ephesians 2:6–7.
[220] Ephesians 3:11.
[221] Ephesians 3:20–21.

Scripture Verses

1 Thessalonians 4:16–17

For the Lord himself shall descend from heaven with a shout, with the voice of the archangel, and with the trump of God: and the dead in Christ shall rise first:

Then we which are alive and remain shall be caught up together with them in the clouds, to meet the Lord in the air: and so shall we ever be with the Lord.

1 Corinthians 6:3

Know ye not that we shall judge angels? how much more things that pertain to this life?

Romans 8:19–23

For the earnest expectation of the creature waiteth for the manifestation of the sons of God.

For the creature was made subject to vanity, not willingly, but by reason of him who hath subjected the same in hope,

Because the creature itself also shall be delivered from the bondage of corruption into the glorious liberty of the children of God.

For we know that the whole creation groaneth and travaileth in pain together until now.

And not only they, but ourselves also, which have the firstfruits of the Spirit, even we ourselves groan within ourselves, waiting for the adoption, to wit, the redemption of our body.

Ephesians 1:23

Which is his body, the fulness of him that filleth all in all.

Ephesians 2:6–7

And hath raised us up together, and made us sit together in heavenly places in Christ Jesus:

That in the ages to come he might shew the exceeding

riches of his grace in his kindness toward us through Christ Jesus.

Ephesians 3:11

According to the eternal purpose which he purposed in Christ Jesus our Lord:

Ephesians 3:20–21

Now unto him that is able to do exceeding abundantly above all that we ask or think, according to the power that worketh in us,

Unto him be glory in the church by Christ Jesus throughout all ages, world without end. Amen.

NOTES

HEBREWS–
REVELATION
Prophecy Resumes

PROPHETIC EVENTS TO COME

M uch of prophecy has already been fulfilled literally by events recorded in the gospels and early Acts. However, much is still left to be fulfilled—most importantly the establishment of the kingdom promised to Israel. (See Romans 11:26–29: "**All Israel shall be saved: As it is written**.")

The following passages make this clear.

Luke 4:17–21

Jesus Christ read a passage from the book Isaiah, closed the book, and said, "This day is this scripture fulfilled in your ears." Compare what He read to the passage in Isaiah 61:1–2 from which He quoted. You will discover that He stopped reading right in the middle of a sentence! He read, "The Spirit of the Lord is upon me, because He hath anointed me to preach the gospel… To preach the acceptable year of the Lord. And He closed the book." But the passage in Isaiah continues in the same sentence with "and the day of vengeance of our God." He did not read that part of the sentence because the day of vengeance (the tribulation) has not yet come.

The Fulfillment of Israel's Feasts (p. 21, Exodus 23, Leviticus 23)

The first group, the Feasts of Passover, Unleavened Bread, and Firstfruits were fulfilled in the crucifixion, burial, and resurrection of Christ. Fifty days later, the Feast of Harvest (also called Pentecost) was fulfilled on the day of Pentecost in Acts 2. But the final group, the Feasts of Trumpets, the Day of Atonement, and the Feast of

Tabernacles (picturing Israel's gathering into her land, national forgiveness, and entrance into the kingdom) have not yet been fulfilled.

Daniel 2

The vision in Daniel 2 pictures the rise and fall of great kingdoms that would rule over Israel. Babylon, Media-Persia, Greece, and Rome all rose and fell consecutively; but the last kingdom, the kingdom of the Antichrist prior to the establishment of God's kingdom, has not yet risen.

THE TRIBULATION

Once this dispensation of grace is over, God will resume the fulfillment of prophecy where it left off in mid-Acts—"the last days"[222] prior to the establishment of the kingdom.

The next event in prophecy is "the time of Jacob's trouble,"[223] the great tribulation. The primary purpose of the tribulation is to be a "refiner's fire" and purge the rebels out of Israel, so that "the offering of Judah and Jerusalem [will] be pleasant to the Lord."[224]

The remnant (true believers in Israel) will go through the fire but not be consumed as was symbolized by the burning bush in Exodus[225] and by Shadrach, Meshach, and Abednego.[226] Believers will know to flee to the mountains of the wilderness where God will provide for them, as He did for their fathers in the Exodus. (See pages 24 and 71.) In fact, Israel's Exodus from Egypt as they fled from Pharaoh is a marvelous picture of Israel's flight from the Antichrist during the tribulation. God will again bare them on eagles' wings. (Compare Exodus 15 and 19:4 with Revelation 12:14–16.)

God will work great signs and wonders through His two witnesses (resurrected Moses and Elijah) and 144,000 Israelites whom He will "seal."[227]

---

[222] Acts 2:16–17; Hebrews 1:1–2.
[223] Jeremiah 30:7.
[224] Malachi 3:2–4; Ezekiel 22:17–22.
[225] Exodus 3:2–3; Malachi 3:6; Isaiah 43:2.
[226] Daniel 3:19+.
[227] Revelation 11:3–7 and 7:4.

Scripture Verses

Acts 2:16–17

But this is that which was spoken by the prophet Joel;

And it shall come to pass in the last days, saith God, I will pour out of my Spirit upon all flesh: and your sons and your daughters shall prophesy, and your young men shall see visions, and your old men shall dream dreams.

Hebrews 1:1–2

God, who at sundry times and in divers manners spake in time past unto the fathers by the prophets,

Hath in these last days spoken unto us by his Son, whom he hath appointed heir of all things, by whom also he made the worlds.

Jeremiah 30:7

Alas! for that day is great, so that none is like it: it is even the time of Jacob's trouble, but he shall be saved out of it.

Malachi 3:2–4

But who may abide the day of his coming? and who shall stand when he appeareth? for he is like a refiner's fire, and like fullers' soap:

And he shall sit as a refiner and purifier of silver: and he shall purify the sons of

Levi, and purge them as gold and silver, that they may offer unto the Lord an offering in righteousness.

Then shall the offering of Judah and Jerusalem be pleasant unto the Lord, as in the days of old, and as in former years.

Ezekiel 22:17–22

And the word of the Lord came unto me, saying,

Son of man, the house of Israel is to me become dross: all they are brass, and tin, and iron, and lead, in the midst of the furnace; they are even the dross of silver.

Therefore thus saith the Lord God; Because ye are all become dross, behold, therefore I will gather you into the midst of Jerusalem.

As they gather silver, and brass, and iron, and lead, and tin, into the midst of the furnace, to blow the fire upon it, to melt it; so will I gather you in mine anger and in my fury, and I will leave you there, and melt you.

Yea, I will gather you, and blow upon you in the fire of my wrath, and ye shall be melted in the midst therof.

As silver is melted in the midst of the furnace, so shall ye be melted in the midst thereof; and ye shall know that I the Lord have poured out my fury upon you.

Exodus 3:2–3

And the angel of the Lord appeared unto him in a flame of fire out of the midst of a bush: and he looked, and, behold, the bush burned with fire, and the bush was not consumed.

And Moses said, I will now turn aside, and see this great sight, why the bush is not burnt.

Malachi 3:6

For I am the Lord, I change not; therefore ye sons of Jacob are not consumed.

Isaiah 43:2

When thou passest through the waters, I will be with thee; and through the rivers, they shall not overflow thee: when thou walkest through the fire, thou shalt not be burned; neither shall the flame kindle upon thee.

Daniel 3:19

Then was Nebuchadnezzar full of fury, and the form of his visage was changed against Shadrach, Meshach, and Abednego: therefore he spake, and commanded that they should heat the furnace one seven times more than it was wont to be heated.

And he commanded the most mighty men that were in his army to bind Shadrach, Meshach, and Abednego, and to cast them into the burning fiery furnace.

Then these men were bound in their coats, their hosen, and their hats, and their other garments, and were cast into the midst of the burning fiery furnace.

Therefore because the king's commandment was urgent, and the furnace exceeding hot, the flames of the fire slew those men that took up Shadrach, Meshach, and Abednego.

And these three men, Shadrach, Meshach, and Abednego, fell down bound into the midst of the burning fiery furnace.

Then Nebuchadnezzar the king was astonished, and rose up in haste, and spake, and said unto his counsellors, Did not we cast three men bound into the midst of the fire?

They answered and said unto the king, True, O king.

He answered and said, Lo, I see four men loose, walking in the midst of the fire, and they have no hurt; and the form of the fourth is like the Son of God.

26 Then Nebuchadnezzar came near to the mouth of the burning fiery furnace, and spake, and said, Shadrach, Meshach, and Abednego, ye servants of the most high God, come forth, and come hither. Then Shadrach, Meshach, and Abednego, came forth of the midst of the fire.

And the princes, governors, and captains, and the king's counsellors, being gathered together, saw these men, upon whose bodies the fire had no power, nor was an hair of their head singed, neither were their coats changed, nor the smell of fire had passed on them.

Then Nebuchadnezzar spake, and said, Blessed be the God of Shadrach, Meshach, and Abednego, who hath sent his angel, and delivered his servants that trusted in him, and have changed the king's word, and yielded their bodies, that they might not serve nor worship any god, except their own God.

Therefore I make a decree, That every people, nation, and language, which speak any thing amiss against the God of Shadrach, Meshach, and Abednego, shall be cut in pieces, and their houses shall be made a dunghill: because there is no other God that can deliver after this sort.

Then the king promoted Shadrach, Meshach, and Abednego, in the province of Babylon.

Revelation 11:3–7

And I will give power unto my two witnesses, and they shall prophesy a thousand two hundred and threescore days, clothed in sackcloth.

These are the two olive trees, and the two candlesticks standing before the God of the earth.

And if any man will hurt them, fire proceedeth out of their mouth, and devoureth their enemies: and if any man will hurt them, he must in this manner be killed.

These have power to shut heaven, that it rain not in the days of their prophecy: and have power over waters to turn them to blood, and to smite the earth with all plagues, as often as they will.

And when they shall have finished their testimony, the beast that ascendeth out of the bottomless pit shall make war against them, and shall overcome them, and kill them.

Revelation 7:4

Of the tribe of Simeon were sealed twelve thousand. Of the tribe of Levi were sealed twelve thousand. Of the tribe of Issachar were sealed twelve thousand.

NOTES

DOCTRINE FOR THE AGES TO COME

After this dispensation of grace, people on earth will need instructions. When Christ was on earth, He taught as if there would be no interruption in the fulfillment of prophecy. Hence, He instructed believers how to prepare for the end times that will precede the establishment of the kingdom.

Those instructions will again apply when prophecy resumes. Matthew 24 is a clear example of this.

The details in the Great Commission at the end of the gospels and the beginning of Acts are also instructions that will be necessary in "the ages to come." Believers then will be empowered with miraculous signs to help them through the tribulation, as Mark 16:16–18 proclaims: "**These signs shall follow** them that believe...cast out devils...new tongues...take up serpents...drink any deadly thing it shall not hurt them." During the tribulation, these signs will be necessary because plagues will be put upon the earth, such as beasts and serpents of the earth being used to kill men[228] and waters being poisoned with wormwood.[229] Also, Israel will need to preach to Jews of all languages, so they will need the gift of tongues, like in Acts 2:6.

This commission will continue into the kingdom following the tribulation, when Israel will become a "kingdom of priests" and will go into all the world and teach the Gentiles as commanded in Matthew 28:19.[230]

---

[228] Revelation 6:8; Jeremiah 8:17 (serpents also symbolize Satan).
[229] Revelation 8:11.
[230] Zechariah 8:23; Isaiah 61:6–9.

In addition, the entire last section of the Bible (Hebrews–Revelation) has "the last days"—the days leading to the establishment of the God's kingdom on earth—in view. (See page 140.)

Scripture Verses

Revelation 6:8

And I looked, and behold a pale horse: and his name that sat on him was Death, and Hell followed with him. And power was given unto them over the fourth part of the earth, to kill with sword, and with hunger, and with death, and with the beasts of the earth.

Jeremiah 8:17

For, behold, I will send serpents, cockatrices, among you, which will not be charmed, and they shall bite you, saith the Lord.

Revelation 8:11

And the name of the star is called Wormwood: and the third part of the waters became wormwood; and many men died of the waters, because they were made bitter.

Zechariah 8:23

Thus saith the Lord of hosts; In those days it shall come to pass, that ten men shall take hold out of all languages of the nations, even shall take hold of the skirt of him that is a Jew, saying, We will go with you: for we have heard that God is with you.

Isaiah 61:6–9

But ye shall be named the Priests of the Lord: men shall call you the Ministers of our God: ye shall eat the riches of the Gentiles, and in their glory shall ye boast yourselves.

For your shame ye shall have double; and for confusion they shall rejoice in their portion: therefore in their land they shall possess the double: everlasting joy shall be unto them.

For I the Lord love judgment, I hate robbery for burnt offering; and I will direct their work in truth, and I will make an everlasting covenant with them.

And their seed shall be known among the Gentiles, and their offspring among the people: all that see them shall acknowledge them, that they are the seed which the Lord hath blessed.

NOTES

HEBREWS–REVELATION

T he books of Hebrews–Revelation focus on and equip believers for the "last days" of the prophetic program. It is marvelous to see that God's Word is laid out in order just as it will work out in history.

Most of these final books were written during the early-Acts time period, before the prophetic fulfillment was interrupted. These books will, therefore, again apply when prophecy resumes. Note a few of the many references in these books to the last days, the tribulation, and the second coming of Christ:

- Hebrews 1:2—"In these last days."
- Hebrews 2:5—"The world to come."
- James 5:8—"The coming of the Lord draweth nigh."
- 1 Peter 1:6–13—"For a season...the trial of your faith... tried with fire...might be found unto praise and honour and glory at the appearing of Jesus Christ."
- 1 Peter 5:8—"The devil, as a roaring lion, walketh about" (See Revelation 12:12–13. Satan is cast to earth during the tribulation.)
- 1 John 2:18—"It is the last time: and as you have heard that antichrist shall come...it is the last time."
- Jude 14–15—"The Lord cometh with ten thousands of his saints, To execute judgment."
- Revelation 1:9—"Your brother, and companion in tribulation and in the kingdom."

ISRAEL IS AGAIN GOD'S PEOPLE

When prophecy resumes, Israel and the earth will again be the focus of God's plans as He fulfills the covenants made with their fathers. (See Romans 11:26–27.)

- **Hebrews** reminds the *Hebrews* of the earthly ministry of Christ and of the Holy Ghost in the apostles in early Acts. It warns them not to neglect the salvation that was confirmed by them with signs and wonders.[231] Hebrews also continually reminds them not to make the same mistake their fathers made with Moses when they did not enter their land because of unbelief.[232] It tells them that if they fall away, it will be impossible to renew them again unto repentance—it will be impossible for them to enter into the kingdom.[233] This is their last chance.
- **James** states quite plainly that he is writing to "the twelve tribes which are scattered abroad."[234] Remember, God had scattered Israel among the nations because of their disobedience and idolatry.[235]
- **Peter** also says he is writing to the "scattered."[236] He tells his audience they are "a royal priesthood" and a "holy nation" just as God said Israel would be.[237]

---

[231] Hebrews 2:1–4.
[232] Hebrews 3:7–18.
[233] Hebrews 6:4–6.
[234] James 1:1.
[235] Leviticus 26:33–39; Jeremiah 50:17; Ezekiel 36:19.
[236] 1 Peter 1:1.
[237] 1 Peter 2:9; Exodus 19:5–6.

- **John** says he is "your brother, and companion in tribulation, and in the kingdom."[238]

James, Peter, and John agreed to confine their ministry to the circumcision.[239]

---

[238] Revelation 1:9.
[239] Galatians 2:9.

Scripture Verses

Hebrews 2:1–4

Therefore we ought to give the more earnest heed to the things which we have heard, lest at any time we should let them slip.

For if the word spoken by angels was stedfast, and every transgression and disobedience received a just recompence of reward;

How shall we escape, if we neglect so great salvation; which at the first began to be spoken by the Lord, and was confirmed unto us by them that heard him;

God also bearing them witness, both with signs and wonders, and with divers miracles, and gifts of the Holy Ghost, according to his own will?

Hebrews 3:7–18

Wherefore (as the Holy Ghost saith, To day if ye will hear his voice,

Harden not your hearts, as in the provocation, in the day of temptation in the wilderness:

When your fathers tempted me, proved me, and saw my works forty years.

Wherefore I was grieved with that generation, and said, They do alway err in their heart; and they have not known my ways.

Hebrews 6:4–6

For it is impossible for those who were once enlightened, and have tasted of the heavenly gift, and were made partakers of the Holy Ghost,

And have tasted the good word of God, and the powers of the world to come,

If they shall fall away, to renew them again unto repentance; seeing they crucify to themselves the Son of God afresh, and put him to an open shame.

James 1:1

James, a servant of God and of the Lord Jesus Christ, to the twelve tribes which are scattered abroad, greeting.

Leviticus 26:33–39

And I will scatter you among the heathen, and will draw out a sword after you: and your land shall be desolate, and your cities waste.

Then shall the land enjoy her sabbaths, as long as it lieth desolate, and ye be in your enemies' land; even then shall the land rest, and enjoy her sabbaths.

As long as it lieth desolate it shall rest; because it did not rest in your sabbaths, when ye dwelt upon it.

And upon them that are left alive of you I will send a faintness into their hearts in the lands of their enemies; and the sound of a shaken leaf shall chase them; and they shall flee, as fleeing from a sword; and they shall fall when none pursueth.

And they shall fall one upon another, as it were before a sword, when none pursueth: and ye shall have no power to stand before your enemies.

And ye shall perish among the heathen, and the land of your enemies shall eat you up.

And they that are left of you shall pine away in their iniquity in your enemies' lands; and also in the iniquities of their fathers shall they pine away with them.

Jeremiah 50:17

Israel is a scattered sheep; the lions have driven him away: first the king of Assyria hath devoured him; and last this Nebuchadrezzar king of Babylon hath broken his bones.

Ezekiel 36:19

And I scattered them among the heathen, and they were dispersed through the countries: according to their way and according to their doings I judged them.

1 Peter 1:1

Peter, an apostle of Jesus Christ, to the strangers scattered throughout Pontus, Galatia, Cappadocia, Asia, and Bithynia.

1 Peter 2:9

But ye are a chosen generation, a royal priesthood, an holy nation, a peculiar people; that ye should shew forth the praises of him who hath called you out of darkness into his marvellous light.

Exodus 19:5–6

Now therefore, if ye will obey my voice indeed, and keep my covenant, then ye shall be a peculiar treasure unto me above all people: for all the earth is mine:

And ye shall be unto me a kingdom of priests, and an holy nation. These are the words which thou shalt speak unto the children of Israel.

Revelation 1:9

I John, who also am your brother, and companion in tribulation, and in the kingdom and patience of Jesus Christ, was in the isle that is called Patmos, for the word of God, and for the testimony of Jesus Christ.

Galatians 2:9

And when James, Cephas, and John, who seemed to be pillars, perceived the grace that was given unto me, they gave to me and Barnabas the right hands of fellowship; that we should go unto the heathen, and they unto the circumcision.

NOTES

THE SECOND COMING
OF CHRIST

At the end of the tribulation, Jesus Christ will mount His white horse and return to the earth with His angels to make war with His enemies and establish His kingdom. He will crush the Antichrist and his armies in the great battle of Armageddon.

The beast and the false prophet will be cast into a lake of fire.[240] The devil will be bound in the bottomless pit "that he should deceive the nations no more, till the thousand years should be fulfilled."[241] Unbelievers will be destroyed, and the believing remnant of Israel will be gathered to enter into the kingdom with their sins forever forgiven.[242] (The fulfillment of the Feasts of Trumpets, Atonement, and Tabernacles; see page 63.)

In Matthew 25:31–46, Christ foretold of the judgment of the nations that will also occur at this time. Note that it is based on the Abrahamic covenant (Gen. 12:1–3). Those who blessed Christ's "brethren" (Israel) during the tribulation are blessed and enter the kingdom; those who cursed His "brethren" (Israel) are cursed and cast into everlasting fire.

Believers who died with the hope of the kingdom (the Old Testament saints and believers of the gospels and early Acts) will be resurrected in glorified bodies to enter the kingdom on earth.[243]

---

[240] Revelation 19:11–21.
[241] Revelation 20:1–3.
[242] Matthew 13:40–43; 24:27–31; Ezekiel 36:25–28; 37:21–28; Psalm 37:9; Isaiah 11:11–12.
[243] Matthew 8:11; Matthew 19:28–29.

Scripture Verses

Revelation 19:11–21

And I saw heaven opened, and behold a white horse; and he that sat upon him was called Faithful and True, and in righteousness he doth judge and make war.

His eyes were as a flame of fire, and on his head were many crowns; and he had a name written, that no man knew, but he himself.

And he was clothed with a vesture dipped in blood: and his name is called The Word of God.

And the armies which were in heaven followed him upon white horses, clothed in fine linen, white and clean.

And out of his mouth goeth a sharp sword, that with it he should smite the nations: and he shall rule them with a rod of iron: and he treadeth the winepress of the fierceness and wrath of Almighty God.

And he hath on his vesture and on his thigh a name written, King Of Kings, And Lord Of Lords.

And I saw an angel standing in the sun; and he cried with a loud voice, saying to all the fowls that fly in the midst of heaven, Come and gather yourselves together unto the supper of the great God;

That ye may eat the flesh of kings, and the flesh of captains, and the flesh of mighty men, and the flesh of horses, and of them that sit on them, and the flesh of all men, both free and bond, both small and great.

And I saw the beast, and the kings of the earth, and their armies, gathered together to make war against him that sat on the horse, and against his army.

And the beast was taken, and with him the false prophet that wrought miracles before him, with which he deceived them that had received the mark of the beast, and them that worshipped his image. These both were cast alive into a lake of fire burning with brimstone.

And the remnant were slain with the sword of him that sat upon the horse, which sword proceeded out of his mouth: and all the fowls were filled with their flesh.

Revelation 20:1–3

And I saw an angel come down from heaven, having the key of the bottomless pit and a great chain in his hand.

And he laid hold on the dragon, that old serpent, which is the Devil, and Satan, and bound him a thousand years,

And cast him into the bottomless pit, and shut him up, and set a seal upon him, that he should deceive the nations no more, till the thousand years should be fulfilled: and after that he must be loosed a little season.

Matthew 13:40–43

As therefore the tares are gathered and burned in the fire; so shall it be in the end of this world.

The Son of man shall send forth his angels, and they shall gather out of his kingdom all things that offend, and them which do iniquity;

And shall cast them into a furnace of fire: there shall be wailing and gnashing of teeth.

Then shall the righteous shine forth as the sun in the kingdom of their Father. Who hath ears to hear, let him hear.

Matthew 24:27–31

For as the lightning cometh out of the east, and shineth even unto the west; so shall also the coming of the Son of man be.

For wheresoever the carcase is, there will the eagles be gathered together.

Immediately after the tribulation of those days shall the sun be darkened, and the moon shall not give her light, and the stars shall fall from heaven, and the powers of the heavens shall be shaken:

And then shall appear the sign of the Son of man in heaven: and then shall all the tribes of the earth mourn, and they shall see the Son of man coming in the clouds of heaven with power and great glory.

And he shall send his angels with a great sound of a trumpet, and they shall gather together his elect from the four winds, from one end of heaven to the other.

Ezekiel 36:25–28

Then will I sprinkle clean water upon you, and ye shall be clean: from all your filthiness, and from all your idols, will I cleanse you.

A new heart also will I give you, and a new spirit will I put within you: and I will take away the stony heart out of your flesh, and I will give you an heart of flesh.

And I will put my spirit within you, and cause you to walk in my statutes, and ye shall keep my judgments, and do them.

And ye shall dwell in the land that I gave to your fathers; and ye shall be my people, and I will be your God.

Ezekiel 37:21–28

And say unto them, Thus saith the Lord God; Behold, I will take the children of Israel from among the heathen, whither they be gone, and will gather them on every side, and bring them into their own land:

And I will make them one nation in the land upon the mountains of Israel; and one king shall be king to them all: and they shall be no more two nations, neither shall they be divided into two kingdoms any more at all.

Neither shall they defile themselves any more with their idols, nor with their detestable things, nor with any of their transgressions: but I will save them out of all their dwelling-places, wherein they have sinned, and will cleanse them: so shall they be my people, and I will be their God.

And David my servant shall be king over them; and they all shall have one shepherd: they shall also walk in my judgments, and observe my statutes, and do them.

And they shall dwell in the land that I have given unto Jacob my servant, wherein your fathers have dwelt; and they shall dwell therein, even they, and their children, and their children's children for ever: and my servant David shall be their prince for ever.

Moreover I will make a covenant of peace with them; it shall be an everlasting covenant with them: and I will place them, and multiply them, and will set my sanctuary in the midst of them for evermore.

My tabernacle also shall be with them: yea, I will be their God, and they shall be my people.

And the heathen shall know that I the Lord do sanctify Israel, when my sanctuary shall be in the midst of them for evermore.

Psalm 37:9

For evildoers shall be cut off: but those that wait upon the Lord, they shall inherit the earth.

Isaiah 11:11–12

And it shall come to pass in that day, that the Lord shall set his hand again the second time to recover the remnant of his people, which shall be left, from Assyria, and from Egypt, and from Pathros, and from Cush, and from Elam, and from Shinar, and from Hamath, and from the islands of the sea.

And he shall set up an ensign for the nations, and shall assemble the outcasts of Israel, and gather together the dispersed of Judah from the four corners of the earth.

Matthew 8:11

And I say unto you, That many shall come from the east and west, and shall sit down with Abraham, and Isaac, and Jacob, in the kingdom of heaven.

Matthew 19:28–29

And Jesus said unto them, Verily I say unto you, That ye which have followed me, in the regeneration when the Son of man shall sit in the throne of his glory, ye also shall sit upon twelve thrones, judging the twelve tribes of Israel.

And every one that hath forsaken houses, or brethren, or sisters, or father, or mother, or wife, or children, or lands, for my name's sake, shall receive an hundredfold, and shall inherit everlasting life.

NOTES

THE THOUSAND-YEAR REIGN OF CHRIST

After the tribulation and second coming, the thousand-year reign of Christ will begin. Satan will be bound in the bottomless pit.[244] Christ will be king over all the earth, ruling from Jerusalem. He will rule with perfect righteousness.[245]

The twelve apostles will sit on twelve thrones judging the twelve tribes of Israel.[246] Israel will finally be gathered and possess the land promised to Abraham, Isaac, and Jacob.[247] They will be under the new covenant and have the law written upon their hearts. God will do in them what they could not do in their own strength—keep the law.[248] The standards Christ taught in Matthew 5 when He magnified the law will be upheld.

Israel will be a light to the Gentiles—the kingdom of priests and ministers of God—that God created them to be.[249] Gentiles who want to be blessed will have to follow the law, keep the feasts, bless Israel, and seek the Lord in Jerusalem.[250]

---

[244] Revelation 20:2–3.
[245] Zechariah 8:3 and 14:9; Isaiah 9:6–7 and 11:4–5; Jeremiah 23:5 and 33:14–16.
[246] Matthew 19:28; Isaiah 1:26.
[247] Jeremiah 23:3–8; Ezekiel 37:21–28 and 20:40–42.
[248] Jeremiah 31:31–38; Ezekiel 36:22–29.
[249] Isaiah 61:6–9; Isaiah 60:2–3, 14.
[250] Isaiah 2:2–4; Zechariah 8:21–23 and 14:16–18; Isaiah 60:3, 5, 12–16; Matthew 5:19–20.

During this time, the curse will be removed from the earth. The land of Israel will be like the garden of Eden. The blind will see, the deaf shall hear, the lame walk, the dumb sing, the parched ground shall become a pool, the wolf shall dwell with the lamb...[251]

---

[251]   Ezekiel 36:34–35; Isaiah 11:6–7.

Scripture Verses

Revelation 20:2–3

And cast him into the bottomless pit, and shut him up, and set a seal upon him, that he should deceive the nations no more, till the thousand years should be fulfilled: and after that he must be loosed a little season.

And when the thousand years are expired, Satan shall be loosed out of his prison.

Zechariah 8:3

Thus saith the Lord; I am returned unto Zion, and will dwell in the midst of Jerusalem: and Jerusalem shall be called a city of truth; and the mountain of the Lord of hosts the holy mountain.

Zechariah 14:9

And the Lord shall be king over all the earth: in that day shall there be one Lord, and his name one.

Isaiah 9:6–7

For unto us a child is born, unto us a son is given: and the government shall be upon his shoulder: and his name shall be called Wonderful, Counsellor, The mighty God, The everlasting Father, The Prince of Peace.

Of the increase of his government and peace there shall be no end, upon the throne of David, and upon his kingdom, to order it, and to establish it with judgment and with justice from henceforth even for ever. The zeal of the Lord of hosts will perform this.

Isaiah 11:4–5

But with righteousness shall he judge the poor, and reprove with equity for the meek of the earth: and he shall smite the earth: with the rod of his mouth, and with the breath of his lips shall he slay the wicked.

And righteousness shall be the girdle of his loins, and faithfulness the girdle of his reins.

Jeremiah 23:5

Behold, the days come, saith the Lord, that I will raise unto David a righteous Branch, and a King shall reign and prosper, and shall execute judgment and justice in the earth.

Jeremiah 33:14–16

Behold, the days come, saith the Lord, that I will perform that good thing which I have promised unto the house of Israel and to the house of Judah.

In those days, and at that time, will I cause the Branch of righteousness to grow up unto David; and he shall execute judgment and righteousness in the land.

In those days shall Judah be saved, and Jerusalem shall dwell safely: and this is the name wherewith she shall be called, The Lord our righteousness.

Matthew 19:28

And Jesus said unto them, Verily I say unto you, That ye which have followed me, in the regeneration when the Son of man shall sit in the throne of his glory, ye also shall sit upon twelve thrones, judging the twelve tribes of Israel.

Isaiah 1:26

And I will restore thy judges as at the first, and thy counsellors as at the beginning: afterward thou shalt be called, The city of righteousness, the faithful city.

Jeremiah 23:3–8

And I will gather the remnant of my flock out of all countries whither I have driven them, and will bring them again to their folds; and they shall be fruitful and increase.

And I will set up shepherds over them which shall feed them: and they shall fear no more, nor be dismayed, neither shall they be lacking, saith the Lord.

Behold, the days come, saith the Lord, that I will raise unto David a righteous Branch, and a King shall reign and prosper, and shall execute judgment and justice in the earth.

In his days Judah shall be saved, and Israel shall dwell safely: and this is his name whereby he shall be called, The Lord Our Righteousness.

Therefore, behold, the days come, saith the Lord, that they shall no more say, The Lord liveth, which brought up the children of Israel out of the land of Egypt;

But, The Lord liveth, which brought up and which led the seed of the house of Israel out of the north country, and from all countries whither I had driven them; and they shall dwell in their own land.

Ezekiel 37:21–28

And say unto them, Thus saith the Lord God; Behold, I will take the children of Israel from among the heathen, whither they be gone, and will gather them on every side, and bring them into their own land:

And I will make them one nation in the land upon the mountains of Israel; and one king shall be king to them all: and they shall be no more two nations, neither shall they be divided into two kingdoms any more at all.

Neither shall they defile themselves any more with their idols, nor with their detestable things, nor with any of their transgressions: but I will save them out of all their dwelling-places, wherein they have sinned, and will cleanse them: so shall they be my people, and I will be their God.

And David my servant shall be king over them; and they all shall have one shepherd: they shall also walk in my judgments, and observe my statutes, and do them.

And they shall dwell in the land that I have given unto Jacob my servant, wherein your fathers have dwelt; and they shall dwell therein, even they, and their children, and their children's children for ever: and my servant David shall be their prince for ever.

Moreover I will make a covenant of peace with them; it shall be an everlasting covenant with them: and I will place them, and multiply them, and will set my sanctuary in the midst of them for evermore.

My tabernacle also shall be with them: yea, I will be their God, and they shall be my people.

And the heathen shall know that I the Lord do sanctify Israel, when my sanctuary shall be in the midst of them for evermore.

Ezekiel 20:40–42

For in mine holy mountain, in the mountain of the height of Israel, saith the Lord God, there shall all the house of Israel, all of them in the land, serve me: there will I accept them, and there will I require your offerings, and the firstfruits of your oblations, with all your holy things.

I will accept you with your sweet savour, when I bring you out from the people, and gather you out of the countries wherein ye have been scattered; and I will be sanctified in you before the heathen.

And ye shall know that I am the Lord, when I shall bring you into the land of Israel, into the country for the which I lifted up mine hand to give it to your fathers.

Jeremiah 31:31–38

Behold, the days come, saith the Lord, that I will make a new covenant with the house of Israel, and with the house of Judah:

Not according to the covenant that I made with their fathers in the day that I took them by the hand to bring them out of the land of Egypt; which my covenant they brake, although I was an husband unto them, saith the Lord:

But this shall be the covenant that I will make with the house of Israel; After those days, saith the Lord, I will put my law in their inward parts, and write it in their hearts; and will be their God, and they shall be my people.

And they shall teach no more every man his neighbour, and every man his brother, saying, Know the Lord: for they shall all know me, from the least of them unto the greatest of them, saith the Lord: for I will forgive their iniquity, and I will remember their sin no more.

Thus saith the Lord, which giveth the sun for a light by day, and the ordinances of the moon and of the stars for a light by night, which divideth the sea when the waves thereof roar; The Lord of hosts is his name:

If those ordinances depart from before me, saith the Lord, then the seed of Israel also shall cease from being a nation before me for ever.

Thus saith the Lord; If heaven above can be measured, and the foundations of the earth searched out beneath, I will also cast off all the seed of Israel for all that they have done, saith the Lord.

Behold, the days come, saith the Lord, that the city shall be built to the Lord from the tower of Hananeel unto the gate of the corner.

Ezekiel 36:22–29

Therefore say unto the house of Israel, thus saith the Lord God; I do not this for your sakes, O house of Israel, but for mine holy name's sake, which ye have profaned among the heathen, whither ye went.

And I will sanctify my great name, which was profaned among the heathen, which ye have profaned in the midst of them; and the heathen shall know that I am the Lord, saith the Lord God, when I shall be sanctified in you before their eyes.

For I will take you from among the heathen, and gather you out of all countries, and will bring you into your own land.

Then will I sprinkle clean water upon you, and ye shall be clean: from all your filthiness, and from all your idols, will I cleanse you.

A new heart also will I give you, and a new spirit will I put within you: and I will take away the stony heart out of your flesh, and I will give you an heart of flesh.

And I will put my spirit within you, and cause you to walk in my statutes, and ye shall keep my judgments, and do them.

And ye shall dwell in the land that I gave to your fathers; and ye shall be my people, and I will be your God.

I will also save you from all your uncleannesses: and I will call for the corn, and will increase it, and lay no famine upon you.

Isaiah 61:6–9

But ye shall be named the Priests of the Lord: men shall call you the Ministers of our God: ye shall eat the riches of the Gentiles, and in their glory shall ye boast yourselves.

For your shame ye shall have double; and for confusion they shall rejoice in their portion: therefore in their land they shall possess the double: everlasting joy shall be unto them.

For I the Lord love judgment, I hate robbery for burnt offering; and I will direct their work in truth, and I will make an everlasting covenant with them.

And their seed shall be known among the Gentiles, and their offspring among the people: all that see them shall acknowledge them, that they are the seed which the Lord hath blessed.

Isaiah 60:2–3, 14

For, behold, the darkness shall cover the earth, and gross darkness the people: but the Lord shall arise upon thee, and his glory shall be seen upon thee.

And the Gentiles shall come to thy light, and kings to the brightness of thy rising.

The sons also of them that afflicted thee shall come bending unto thee; and all they that despised thee shall bow themselves down at the soles of thy feet; and they shall call thee; The city of the Lord, The Zion of the Holy One of Israel.

Isaiah 2:2–4

And it shall come to pass in the last days, that the mountain of the Lord's house shall be established in the top of the mountains, and shall be exalted above the hills; and all nations shall flow unto it.

And many people shall go and say, Come ye, and let us go up to the mountain of the Lord, to the house of the God of Jacob; and he will teach us of his ways, and we will walk in his paths: for out of Zion shall go forth the law, and the word of the Lord from Jerusalem.

And he shall judge among the nations, and shall rebuke many people: and they shall beat their swords into plowshares, and their spears into pruninghooks: nation shall not lift up sword against nation, neither shall they learn war any more.

Zechariah 8:21–23

And the inhabitants of one city shall go to another, saying, Let us go speedily to pray before the Lord, and to seek the Lord of hosts: I will go also.

Yea, many people and strong nations shall come to seek the Lord of hosts in Jerusalem, and to pray before the Lord.

Thus saith the Lord of hosts; In those days it shall come to pass, that ten men shall take hold out of all languages of the nations, even shall take hold of the skirt of him that is a Jew, saying, We will go with you: for we have heard that God is with you.

Zechariah 14:16–18

And it shall come to pass, that every one that is left of all the nations which came against Jerusalem shall even go up from year to year to worship the King, the Lord of hosts, and to keep the feast of tabernacles.

And it shall be, that whoso will not come up of all the families of the earth unto Jerusalem to worship the King, the Lord of hosts, even upon them shall be no rain.

And if the family of Egypt go not up, and come not, that have no rain; there shall be the plague, wherewith the Lord will smite the heathen that come not up to keep the feast of tabernacles.

Isaiah 60:3, 5, 12–16

And the Gentiles shall come to thy light, and kings to the brightness of thy rising.

Then thou shalt see, and flow together, and thine heart shall fear, and be enlarged; because the abundance of the sea shall be converted unto thee, the forces of the Gentiles shall come unto thee.

For the nation and kingdom that will not serve thee shall perish; yea, those nations shall be utterly wasted.

The glory of Lebanon shall come unto thee, the fir tree, the pine tree, and the box together, to beautify the place of my sanctuary; and I will make the place of my feet glorious.

The sons also of them that afflicted thee shall come bending unto thee; and all they that despised thee shall bow themselves down at the soles of thy feet; and they shall call thee; The city of the Lord, The Zion of the Holy One of Israel.

Whereas thou has been forsaken and hated, so that no man went through thee, I will make thee an eternal excellency, a joy of many generations.

Thou shalt also suck the milk of the Gentiles, and shalt suck the breast of kings: and thou shalt know that I the Lord am thy Saviour and thy Redeemer, the mighty One of Jacob.

Matthew 5:19–20

Whosoever therefore shall break one of these least commandments, and shall teach men so, he shall be called the least in the kingdom of heaven: but whosoever shall do and teach them, the same shall be called great in the kingdom of heaven.

For I say unto you, That except your righteousness shall exceed the righteousness of the scribes and Pharisees, ye shall in no case enter into the kingdom of heaven.

Ezekiel 36:34–35

And the desolate land shall be tilled, whereas it lay desolate in the sight of all that passed by.

And they shall say, This land that was desolate is become like the garden of Eden; and the waste and desolate and ruined cities are become fenced, and are inhabited.

Isaiah 11:6–7

The wolf also shall dwell with the lamb, and the leopard shall lie down with the kid; and the calf and the young lion and the fatling together; and a little child shall lead them.

And the cow and the bear shall feed; their young ones shall lie down together: and the lion shall eat straw like the ox.

NOTES

The New Heaven and New Earth
The Dispensation of the Fullness of Times

At the end of the one thousand years, Satan will be loosed for a season. He will again deceive the nations.[252] There will be one final battle between the Lord and Satan and those who followed him. The Lord will be victorious. The Lord's enemies will be devoured by a great fire out of heaven, and Satan will be cast into the lake of fire forever.[253]

After this, the "great white throne" of judgment will occur. This is the final judgment of all unbelievers. They will be judged according to what is written in "the books" (the Bible) and the book of life. Ultimately, they are cast into the lake of fire with death and hell.[254]

There will be "a new heaven and a new earth."[255] The body of Christ will have already been ruling with Christ in heaven. The holy city, the new Jerusalem, will descend from God out of heaven. It will have twelve gates with the names of the twelve tribes of Israel and twelve foundations with the names of the twelve apostles.[256] God, in the person of Jesus Christ, will rule the earth from new Jerusalem through redeemed Israel forever.

---

[252] Revelation 20: 3, 7.
[253] Revelation 20:9–10.
[254] Revelation 20:11–15.
[255] Revelation 21:1.
[256] Revelation 21:2, 10–14.

Thus, "the dispensation of the fullness of times" will begin (Eph. 1:10). Jesus Christ will be "the blessed and only Potentate, the King of kings, and Lord of lords"[257] over all of creation, both in heaven and earth. Israel will be ruling with Christ on earth; the body of Christ will be ruling with Him in heaven.

> *All things will be "gathered together in one...*
> in Christ, *both which are in heaven and which are*
> *on earth; even in Him"* (Eph. 1:10).

---

[257] 1 Timothy 6:15.

Scripture Verses

Revelation 20:3, 7

And cast him into the bottomless pit, and shut him up, and set a seal upon him, that he should deceive the nations no more, till the thousand years should be fulfilled: and after that he must be loosed a little season.

And when the thousand years are expired, Satan shall be loosed out of his prison,

Revelation 20:9–10

And they went up on the breadth of the earth, and compassed the camp of the saints about, and the beloved city: and fire came down from God out of heaven, and devoured them.

And the devil that deceived them was cast into the lake of fire and brimstone, where the beast and the false prophet are, and shall be tormented day and night for ever and ever.

Revelation 20:11–15

And I saw a great white throne, and him that sat on it, from whose face the earth and the heaven fled away; and there was found no place for them.

And I saw the dead, small and great, stand before God; and the books were opened: and another book was opened, which is the book of life: and the dead were judged out of those things which were written in the books, according to their works.

And the sea gave up the dead which were in it; and death and hell delivered up the dead which were in them: and they were judged every man according to their works.

And death and hell were cast into the lake of fire. This is the second death.

And whosoever was not found written in the book of life was cast into the lake of fire.

Revelation 21:1

And I saw a new heaven and a new earth: for the first heaven and the first earth were passed away; and there was no more sea.

Revelation 21:2, 10–14

And I John saw the holy city, new Jerusalem, coming down from God out of heaven, prepared as a bride adorned for her husband.

And he carried me away in the spirit to a great and high mountain, and shewed me that great city, the holy Jerusalem, descending out of heaven from God,

Having the glory of God: and her light was like unto a stone most precious, even like a jasper stone, clear as crystal;

And had a wall great and high, and had twelve gates, and at the gates twelve angels, and names written thereon, which are the names of the twelve tribes of the children of Israel:

On the east three gates; on the north three gates; on the south three gates; and on the west three gates.

And the wall of the city had twelve foundations, and in them the names of the twelve apostles of the Lamb.

1 Timothy 6:15

Which in his times he shall shew, who is the blessed and only Potentate, the King of kings, and Lord of lords.

Thou art worthy, O Lord, to receive glory and honour and power: for thou hast created all things, and for thy pleasure they are and were created.
                                                    —Revelation 4:11

New Heaven and New Earth

ABOUT THE AUTHOR

G reg, a Christian for over 20 years, is a clear example of how God can use ordinary, imperfect people to do amazing things.

Greg is a husband and father of a wonderful wife and two amazing children. It is clear that not only did God guide him through the gauntlets of life and business but in the end richly blessed him with a life and family he always wanted.

Greg has demonstrated his heart to serve not only his local church but many other National and International ministries such as;

Forgotten Truths, www.forgottentruths.com) a national TV broadcast of Pastor Richard Jordan, President of Grace School of Bible that teaches the word of God according to God's instruction which is II Timothy 2:15, "rightly dividing the word of truth",

Global Media Outreach, (www.globalmediaoutreach.com) an International internet ministry that is literally harvesting thousands of decisions for Christ every day around the world,

Samaritans Purse National disaster relief ministry (www.samaratanspurse.org) that is first to arrive all around the United States when any large scale National Disaster hits to provide life essentials to the local community.

Trellis, Costa Mesa, CA.,(www.wearetrellis.com) is an organization dedicated to bringing the Christian church community of all denominations together to make a difference in our collective community on many fronts including homelessness, after school mentoring of elementary children that come from families where English is the second language, and a city-wide event called Love Costa Mesa, where thousands of volunteers go out and do acts of community service for real people.

Legacy Makers, (www.chooseourlegacy.com) a up and coming 501C3 that is dedicated to helping young families become more intentional in building God-centric family traditions and experiences so that a positive family legacy can be passed on for generations to come. Please check out these ministries and consider supporting them.

In the end, I believe God will say to Greg, "well done" you have given your time, talent, and treasure to spread the good news about Jesus to any who would listen.

CPSIA information can be obtained
at www.ICGtesting.com
Printed in the USA
FSHW012045141021